CYNON VALLEY PLACE-NAMES

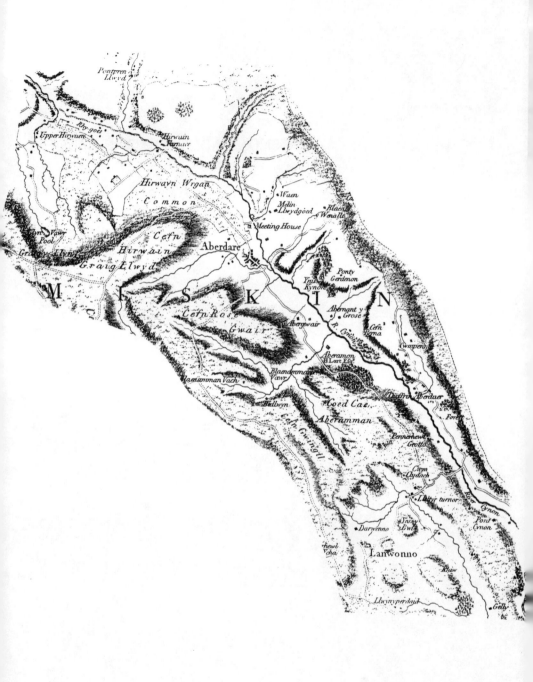

Pontyren
Llwyd

Rhy goes
Upper Hirwaen

Hirwain
Furnace

Hirwaun Wrgan

Common

Waen

Melin
Llwydgoed

Ca

Blaen
Wonalla

Cefn

Meeting House

Hirwain

Aberdare

Graig Llwyn
Vawr
Pool

Graig Llwyd

Graig Llwyd

Cefn Ros

Ponty
Gardenon

Ynys
Kynon

M   S   K   I   N

Gwair

Abergwair

Abernant y
Grose

R. Cynon

Cefn
Pena

Wnypew

Aberaman
H Lort Efst

Blaenymman
Vawr

Faestimman Vach

Balbyn

Coed Cae

Dduffrn Bodaer

Forest

Aberamman

Pennenewl
Grotto

Chwm
Llydnch

Darwenno

Ynysy
Bwl

Lhdor turnor

Riwr Cynon

Pont
Cynon

Chewl
Cha

Lanwonno

Rhiw

Llwynyperdaid

Gelli

Cynon Valley
Place-Names

Deric John

ISBN: 0-86381-472-7

Cover design: Alan Jones

First published in 1998 by Gwasg Carreg Gwalch,
12 Iard yr Orsaf, Llanrwst, Wales LL26 0EH
☎ (01492) 642031
Printed and published in Wales.

Deric John

A former schoolmaster at Lansdowne Road Junior School Cardiff and at Vaynor and Penderyn Comprehensive School Cefncoedycymer, Deric, since his early retirement, has been actively involved in place-name research and etymology. He is a member of the English Place-name Society (unfortunately there is no Welsh Place-name Society) and regularly contributes articles on place-names to '*Clochdar*', the Cynon Valley Welsh Language newspaper, and to '*Siglen*', the Mensans' Welsh Language periodical. Born in Pontarddulais, he has resided in the Cynon Valley since 1971, and over the years, many of our residents have been involved with his Adult Welsh Language classes at Penderyn, Mountain Ash and Blaen-gwawr. It is as a result of the demand by former pupils, students and friends for information on the place-names of the valley that Deric has decided to publish his research. Any profits will be donated to local charities.

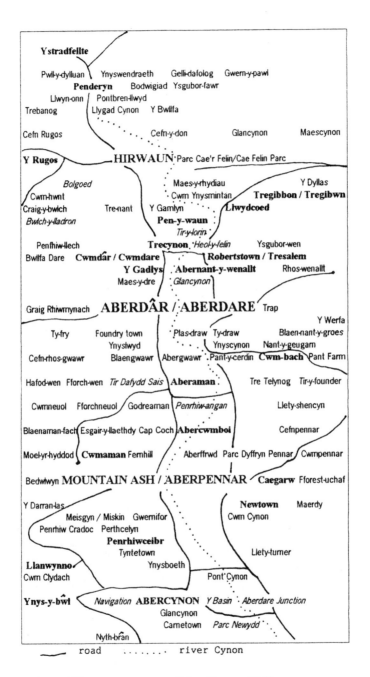

Ystradfellte

Pwll-y-dylluan Ynyswendraeth Gelli-dafolog Gwern-y-pawl
Penderyn Bodwigiad Ysgubor-fawr
Llwyn-onn Pontbren-llwyd
Trebanog Llygad Cynon Y Bwllfa

Cefn Rugos Cefn-y-don Glancynon Maescynon

Y Rugos **HIRWAUN** Parc Cae'r Felin/Cae Felin Parc

Bolgoed Maes-y-rhydiau Y Dyllas
Cwm-hwnt Cwm Ynysmintan **Tregibbon / Tregibwn**
Craig-y-bwlch Tre-nant Y Gamlyn **Llwydcoed**
Bwlch-y-lladron **Pen-y-waun**
Tir-y-lorin
Penrhiw-llech **Trecynon** *Heol-y-felin* Ysgubor-wen
Bwllfa Dare **Cwmdâr / Cwmdare** **Robertstown / Tresalem**
Y Gadlys Abernant-y-wenallt Rhos-wenallt
Maes-y-dre *Glancynon*

Graig Rhiwrmynach **ABERDÂR / ABERDARE** Trap

Y Werfa
Ty-fry Foundry town Plas-draw Ty-draw Blaen-nant-y-groes
Ynyslwyd Ynyscynon Nant-y-geugarn
Cefn-rhos-gwawr Blaengwawr Abergwawr Pant-y-cerdin **Cwm-bach** Pant Farm

Hafod-wen Fforch-wen *Tir Dafydd Sais* **Aberaman** Tre Telynog Tir-y-founder

Cwmneuol Fforchneuol Godreaman *Penrhiw-angan* Llety-shencyn

Blaenaman-fach Esgair-y-llaethdy Cap Coch **Abercwmboi** Cefnpennar

Moel-yr-hyddod **Cwmaman** Fernhill Aberffrwd Parc Dyffryn Pennar Cwmpennar

Bedwlwyn **MOUNTAIN ASH / ABERPENNAR** Caegarw Fforest-uchaf

Y Darran-las **Newtown** Maerdy
Meisgyn / Miskin Gwernifor Cwm Cynon
Penrhiw Cradoc Perthcelyn
Penrhiwceibr
Tyntetown Llety-turner
Llanwynno Ynysboeth
Cwm Clydach Pont Cynon

Ynys-y-bŵl *Navigation* **ABERCYNON** Y Basin *Aberdare Junction*
Glancynon
Carnetown *Parc Newydd*
Nyth-brân

——— road .... river Cynon

Place-name map of the Cynon Valley.

Drawing of Pont Cynon near Abercynon by Emma Bacon c.1828. Emma and Lucy Bacon were grand-daughters of Anthony Bacon II the celebrated iron master and founder of the Cyfarchfa Works, Merthyr Tydfil.
He lived in Aberaman House until his death in 1827.
Drawing from the Bacon Collection by kind permission of Aberdare Library.

The site of the demolished Cwm Cynon Colliery 1996 overlooking Miskin with Newtown and Fforest Uchaf in the background.

Tafarn y Blaengwawr takes its name from the headwater of the Gwawr brook.

PREFACE

Place-names are an integral part of the world in which we live, be they names of towns and villages, names of features in the landscape, or names of streets and houses. We describe our environment by the names which we give to its features and thus we are able to recognise our communities which we share together. The names may be strictly descriptive topographically - the meeting place of two streams, the nature of the terrain, some outstanding feature; they may be facetious, or denote ownership or usage, but they all had, at the time of naming, some significance.

Place-names have meaning beyond the dictionary definitions of their elements. Place-names have, for that reason, been called 'sign-posts to the past' because discovering their deeper significance can tell us so much about a variety of topics - farming practices, enclosures, the coming of industrialisation, boundaries, ownership and tenancies, changes in the environment, the nature of society. Places are named in the language of the community and thus they are able to speak to us across the centuries of changes in that language and its dialects.

In his detailed explanations of the names of towns, villages, hamlets and residences in the Cynon valley Deric John has provided us with very effective sign-posts to our local history. He begins with the meaning (and pronounciation and correct spelling) of each place-name. This in itself is no easy task given the variety of forms which exist and which are carefully noted and dated here, but it is the essential first step, especially in a community where Welsh is no longer the predominant language. But he then goes on to show the significance of each name and its variants or alternantives, and the light which these can shed on the knowledge of the history of the development of settlements and industry in the valley. Each entry is an absorbing story.

Over the years place-names change. Some are forgotten because they are no longer required; some are 'corrected' and made respectable (look up Bwlchylladron, Ynysbendorth). Some fall prey to mistaken ideas of being 'with it' and are unfaithful to their roots, but some gain new life as new settlements take on the names of older farms, fields and hamlets. The local authority is to be congratulated on the way it has consistently over the years developed established patterns of names like Tresalem, Tregibwn, Trecynon to create new names like Tre-waun, Tre-nant, Tre-ivor and to safeguard old names in new housing developments in e.g. Ty-fry, Cwmbach and Cwmdare. This is not being sentimental. The task of local history is to link our present with our past, and in that task place-names has a special role to play. The sign-posts to the past are firmly planted in the present; they are symbols of the continuity of society in its own environment.

Deric John has performed a great service for all of us by revealing the secrets of these place-names and by making them so meaningful once again. He has helped us to reclaim our past and to set foundations for a continuing future.

Brynley F.Roberts.

INTRODUCTION

The aim of this work is to provide a means of reference for anyone interested in the meanings of the place-names of the Cynon Valley. Over seventy place-names have been recorded, and where possible, explained. The names are of towns, villages, hamlets and residential areas of the Cynon Valley from Llygad Cynon, Penderyn to Abercynon. Some field-names of the parishes of Aberdare, Llanwynno and Penderyn are also included.

The place-names have been extracted from various sources, such as The Tithe Maps and Schedules of the Parishes of Aberdare, Llanwynno and Penderyn; Parish Registers; Llanwynno Parish Rate Books 1842-50; Ordnance Survey Maps, and I am particularly indebted to three place-name specialists for the work they had previously carried out on this topic in this locality.

I refer to R.J.Thomas and his unpublished M.A. thesis 'Astudiaeth o enwau lleoedd Cwmwd Meisgyn'. 1933. (RJT & Meisg), Dr Brynley F Roberts for his essay 'Some Aberdare Place-names', published by the Cynon Valley History Society 'Old Aberdare',Volume Seven (SAPN) and to R. F. Peter Powell for the information on the place-names of the parish of Penderyn in his book *The Place-names of Devynock Hundred*, (PNBH).

The works of Ifor Williams, Dr Melville Richards, Dr B.G. Charles, Bedwyr Lewis Jones, Gwynedd Pierce, Tomos Roberts, Hywel Wyn Owen and J.Lloyd-Jones on Welsh place-names have been fountains of knowledge, and I have relied greatly on their expertise in this field.

I have also profited from the works of Dr Margaret Gelling, Kenneth Cameron, John Field, Dr Kenneth Jackson, W.F.H.Nicolaisen, Eilert Ekwall, Rivet & Smith, T.J.Morgan and Prys Morgan and others. My membership of the English Place-name Society has also been advantageous.

I thank the staff of Aberdare Library for their diligence and courteousness at all times, as well as the staff of The University of Wales Library, Cardiff, The Cardiff Central Library, the staff at the National Library of Wales, Aberystwyth, the County Archivist, County Hall, Swansea, Tomos Roberts, The Archivist at the University College of

North Wales, Bangor, for the information contained in the Melville Richards place-name cards, Gwynedd Pierce for his advice and material, Tom Evans, Abernant Road for his wealth of local knowledge and to the many friends who have helped me in my endeavours.

I reserve a special thank you for Doctor Brynley F. Roberts as he has given much of his valuable time in reading my original manuscript as well as offering me sound advice and detailed comments. Without his contribution, the work would have been very much the poorer.

My most ardent supporter has been Anita my wife and I thank her deeply for being so patient and considerate, especially when place-names took priority over household chores. I thank my daughter Rhian for buying me my first book on place-names and my son Huw for making me computer semi- (my fault not his) literate.

I have endeavoured to name all sources. Spelling is as
at source. The dates following the place-name indicate
when that form was recorded, followed by the source.

eg. Aberdare. 1203. Margam. 174. RJT. Meisg. 60.

Aberdare is the recorded form.
The year is AD 1203.
The source is the 'History of Margam Abbey', page
174 as recorded by R.J. Thomas in his unpublished
M.A. thesis 'Astudiaeth o Enwau Lleoedd Cwmwd
Meisgyn', page 60.

I have included an aid on pronounciation which might be of help to Welsh learners and non Welsh-speakers.

For a full introduction to place-names in this locality, may I refer you to Dr B.F. Roberts's Some Aberdare Place-names, pages 1-6.

The faults and weaknesses in this work are all my very own.

Deric Meidrum John   Aberdare   1995.

PLACE-NAME ETYMOLOGY

Pitfalls

1. Never take a place-name at its face value.
Always trace the earlier recorded forms of the name. eg. *Merthyr Mawr* was originally *Merthyr Myfor* [Myfor's church]. *Llancaiach* was originally *Glancaiach* [bank of the Caiaich stream]. *Cwmrhydyceirw* was originally *Cwmrhydycwrw* [valley + ford + beer]. *Pont-y-clun* was originally *Pont-y-clown.* [bridge on the river named Clown]. *Ynyswendraeth* was originally *Ynysbendorth* [river meadow of the loaf shaped hill]. *Abercwmboi* was originally *Aber confoi*, [Cynfoi, pers. name] etc.

2. Make sure of the language.
Swansea has nothing to do with Eng. *swan* and *sea* < Norse. Sweyne's eye [Sweyne's isle]. *Flatholme* is not topogrophical Eng. *flat* < Norse Flotholme [fleet isle, home of a Viking fleet]. *Wrexham* has nothing to do with Lat. *rex* < O.E. Wriestelsham > Gwregsam > Wrexham. *Worms Head* is not Eng. *worm* but < O.E. wyrm = snake or dragon. *Gleneagles*, Sco. is not Eng. *eagles* but Cymric *eglwys* < Glenegles (church valley) 1685. (BLJ.). *Eryri* (Snowdonia) is not Welsh for eagles (eryrod) but Welsh for *shingles* (raised lumps on the surface), etc.

3. People transfer names.
eg. Beaupre; Hensol; Bethlehem; Bethel; Bethesda, etc.

4. Beware of popular etymology.
Stories are invented of giants and battles etc. eg. *Penrhys; Y Gadlys* etc. Local toponomysts change the names in order to provide an etymology. eg. *Bwlch y lladron* to *bwlch lled y rhiw*; *Penderyn* to Pendeuryn, Pendarren, Penderi; *Bargod* to Bargoed etc.

5. Words are copied incorrectly; dialect words are not understood; Monoglot scribes have difficulties with the orthography of other languages. etc.

In short, it is a minefield, and one must be ultra careful with every step one takes!

CYNON VALLEY PLACE-NAMES.

1. Abbreviations and Bibliography.

AP.	*Armes Prydein* ed. Sir Ifor Williams, (Dublin, 1982 [1972]).
APP.	*Aberdare, Pictures from the Past* Vol.1,1986.Vol.2,1992. Cynon Valley History Society.
BIBC.	Mary William, *Blas ar Iaith Blaenau'r Cymoedd* (Llyfrau Llafar Gwlad, 18, Llanrwst, 1990).
BWP.	Sir Ifor Williams, *The Beginnings of Welsh Poetry* ed. Rachel Bromwich , (Cardiff, 1990 [1972]).
BWS.	K.M. Evans, *A Book of Welsh Saints* (Penarth, 1959).
CA.	Ifor Williams, *Canu Aneirin* (Caerdydd, 1938).
CED.	*Chambers English Dictionary* 7th ed. 1988.
CELTS.	Henri Hubert, *The Rise of the Celts* (London 1987).
CLlH.	Ifor Williams, *Canu Llywarch Hen* (Caerdydd, 1935).
CM.	Kenneth Jackson, *A Celtic Miscellany* (London, 1951).
CN.	T.F.G. Dexter, *Cornish Names* (Truro, 1968).
Cph.	Iorwerth C. Peate, *Cymru A'i Phobl* (Caerdydd, 1933).
CVAI.	Raymond Grant, *Cynon Valley in the Age of Iron,* (Aberdare, 1991).
CVOH.	*Cynon Valley Official Handbook* (1994).
CWV.	D.D.& J.M. Gladwin, *The Canals of the Welsh Valleys and their Tramroads* Oakwood Press, (Oxford, 1991).
CYFG.	Melville Richards, *Cystrawen Y Frawddeg Gymraeg* (Caerdydd, 1938).
DEE.	T.F. Hoad, *The Concise Oxford Dictionary of English Etymology* (Oxford, 1986).
DYB.	Gwynedd Pierce, *Dan y Bargod* (Prifysgol Cymru, 1990).
DYIG.	Henry Lewis, *Datblygiad Yr Iaith Gymraeg* (Caerdydd, 1931).
EANC.	R.J. Thomas, *Enwau Afonydd a Nentydd Cymru* (Cardiff, 1938).
EEW.	T.H. Parry-Williams, *The English Element in Welsh,* (London, 1923).
EFN.	John Field, *English Field-names, A Dictionary* (Gloucester, 1989[1972]).
Ell.	Ifor Williams, *Enwau Lleoedd* (Liverpool, 1945).
Ell2.	Hywel Wyn Owen, *Enwau Lleoedd* (CAA, Aberystwyth, HMSO, 1990).
ELlAC.	Bedwyr Lewis Jones, *Enwau Lleoedd Abergele a'r Cylch,* (Cymdeithas Emrys Ap Iwan, 1992).
ELlBM.	Richard Morgan, G.G. Evans, *Enwau Lleoedd Buallt a Maesyfed* (Llyfrau Llafar Gwlad.27. Llanrwst, 1993).
ELlSG.	J. Lloyd-Jones, *Enwau Lleoedd Sir Gaernarfon* (Cardiff, 1928).
Eng.PN.	K. Cameron, *English Place-Names* (London, 1969).

ENWAU.   Bedwyr Lewis Jones, *Enwau* (Llyfrau Llafar Gwlad, 20, Llanrwst, 1991).

EPN.   Eilert Ekwall, *A Concise Dictionary of English Place-names* (4th. Edition, Oxford, 1959).

EPNE.   A.H. Smith, *English Place-Name Elements* English Place-Name Society Volume XXV (Cambridge, 1956).

ESCV.   *Environmental Studies in the Cynon Valley* Mid Glamorgan County Council.

EWGP.   Kenneth Jackson, *Early Welsh Gnomic Poems* (Caerdydd, 1935). EWP. Ifor Williams, *Lectures on Early Welsh Poetry*, (Dublin, 1944).

GBGG.   J. Lloyd-Jones, *Geirfa Barddoniaeth Gynnar Gymraeg* (Cardiff, 1931-63).

GA.   Thomas D. Lewellyn, T.J. Jones, (Cynonwyson), *Gardd Aberdar* (1854).

GCBAC.   H.N. Savoury, *Guide Catalogue of the Bronze Age Collections* National Museum of Wales, (Cardiff, 1980).

Geir.Geg.   S. Minwel Tibbott, *Geirfa'r Gegin* (Llandysul, 1993[1983]).

Geir.Glo.   Lynn Davies, *Geirfa'r Glowr* (Llandysul, 1976).

GM.   H. Meurig Evans, W.O. Thomas, *Y Geiriadur Mawr* (Llandybie/Aberystwyth, 3rd edn. 1963).

GPC.   *Geiriadur Prifysgol Cymru* (Cardiff, 1950-).

GWPN.   Elwyn Davies, *A Gazetteer of Welsh Place-Names* (Cardiff, 1967 [1957]).

HC.   John Davies, *Hanes Cymru* (London, 1990).

HC18g.   R.T. Jenkins, *Hanes Cymru yn y Ddeunawfed Ganrif* (Caerdydd, 1945).

HC19g.   R.T. Jenkins, *Hanes Cymru yn y Bedwaredd Ganrif ar Bymtheg* (Caerdydd, 1933.)

HCI.   D.L. Davies, *A History of Cwmaman Institute 1868-1993* (Aberdare, 1994)

HW.   J.E. Lloyd, *A History of Wales* Vol 1. (Llandysul,1989, [1911]).

HMH   Thomas Evans, *The History of Miskin Higher* (Mountain Ash,1946).

HPP.   D. Davies, *Hanes Plwyf Penderyn* (1904).

IaLl.   Melville Richards, "Iaith a Llen", *The Bulletin of the Board of Celtic Studies* Volume XXVI, University of Wales Press, 1976.

ILNE.   P.W. Joyce, *Irish Local Names Explained,* (London, 1990 edn. [1923]).

ISSWW.   Melville Richards, 'Irish Settlements of South West Wales' in *Royal Society of Antiquaries* (based on paper read at the first International Congress of Celtic Studies, at Dublin, July, 1959.

LHEB.   Kenneth Jackson, *Language and History in Early Britain* (Edinburgh, 1953).

14

LL.	*Liber Landavensis* ed J. Gwenogvryn Evans and John Rhys, (Oxford, 1893). [Aberdare Library].
LYH.	Lewis Davies, *Lewsyn Yr Heliwr* (Caernarfon National Eisteddfod, 1921). Wrecsam 1922.
MAP&A.	B. Baldwin & H. Rogers, *Mountain Ash, Penrhiwceiber and Abercynon* The Old Photographs Series, Redwood Books, (Trowbridge, 1994).
Meisg.	R.J. Thomas, *Astudiaeth o Enwau Lleoedd Cwmwd Meisgyn* Unpublished M.A. thesis, (University of Wales, Cardiff, 1933).
MPNGBI.	Adrian Room, *A Concise Dictionary of Modern Place-names in Great Britain and Ireland* (Oxford, 1983).
MIG.	Gwynedd Pierce, 'Mynegbyst i'r Gorffennol' in I.M. Williams (ed.) *Abertawe a'r Cylch* (Llandybie,1968).
MT.	Merthyr Teacher Centre Group, *Merthyr Tydfil* (Cowbridge, 1981).
NTCB.	Gelling, M., Nicolaisen W.F.H., Richards M., *The Names of Towns and Cities in Britain* (London, 1970).
OA.	*Old Aberdare* Cynon Valley History Society. Vol 1 - V11. (1976-1993).
OBWV.	*The Oxford Book of Welsh Verse* ed. Thomas Parry (Oxford, 1962).
ODECN.	E.C. Withycombe, *The Oxford Dictionary of English Christian Names* (Oxford, 1950).
OSM.	Ordnance Survey Map.
PDS.	Basil Cottle, *The Penguin Dictionary of Surnames* (Penguin Books, 1967).
Pen.	Nansi Selwood, *Penderyn,a History* (1990).
PHG.	Raymond Grant, *The Parliamentary History of Glamorgan 1542-1976* (Swansea, 1978).
PNBI.	Adrian Room, *Dictionary of Place-names in the British Isles* (London, 1988).
PNC,Bangor.	Melville Richards' place-name cards Bangor, courtesy of Tomos Roberts.
PNDH.	R.F. Peter Powell, *The Place-names of Devynock Hundred* (published by the author, 1993).
PNDPH.	Gwynedd O. Pierce, *The Place-names of Dinas Powys Hundred* (Cardiff, 1968).
PNG.	H.C. Jones, *Place-names in Glamorgan* (Risca, 1976).
PNGBI.	John Field, *Place-names of Great Britain and Ireland* (Newton Abbott 1980).
PNL.	Margaret Gelling, *Place-names in the Landscape* (London, 1993[1984]).
PNP.	B.G. Charles, *The Place-names of Pembrokeshire* (Aberystwyth, 1992).

PNRB.   Rivet, A.L.F., Smith, C., *The Place-names of Roman Britain*
            (London, 1981).
PS.   Plymouth Surveys 1766. (Taken from 'Meisg.').
RDPN.   Richards, M., Williams, I., contributors to 'Place-names' in
            The Reader's Digest Complete Atlas of the British Isles (1965).
RNEW.   The Royal National Eisteddfod of Wales.
RR.   Rent Roll. circ.1700. (Taken from 'Meisg.').
SA.   Thomas Evans, *The Story of Abercynon* 2nd.ed.
            (Tonypandy,1955).
SAPN.   Brynley F. Roberts, 'Some Aberdare Place-names', in
            Old Aberdare Vol.VII (Cynon Valley History Society,1993).
SEHB.   Pauline Gregg, *A Social and Economic History of Britain
            1760-1960,* (London, 1962).
SPNs.   W.F.H. Nicolaisen, *Scottish Place-names* (London,1979).
Spurrell.   *Spurrell's English-Welsh and Welsh-English Dictionary* ed.
            J. Bodvan Anwyl.1926 edn. (Carmarthen,1913).
STTP.   Margaret Gelling, *Signposts to the Past* (London,1978).
TAG.   Melville Richards, 'Enwau Lleoedd - Tir a gwlad', in *Y Cymro*,
            166 weekly articles written 27th March, 1967 - 27th May, 1970.
TM.   Tithe Map.
TMC.   Michael Eyers, *The Masters of the Coalfield* (Risca,Gwent,1992).
TS.   Tithe Schedules.
WVF.   D. Dykes, *Wales in Vanity Fair* Nat.Museum Wales,
            (Cardiff,1989).
WL.   Janet Davies, *The Welsh Language* (Cardiff,1993).
WM.   Ditectif Geiriau. Place-name articles written in the
            Western Mail. (1991 -). Contributors have included, Bedwyr
            Lewis Jones, Hywel Wyn Owen, Gwynedd O. Pierce and Tomos
            Roberts.
WPELVE.   J. Vyrnwy Morgan, *Welsh Political and Educational Leaders in
            the Victorian Era* (London,1908).
Wpns.   Dewi Davies, *Welsh Place-names And Their Meanings*
            (Aberystwyth, c.1975).
WPnsB.   Dewi Davies, *Welsh Place-names of Breconshire* (Brecon,1971).
W.Srns.   Morgan, T.J., Morgan, Prys, *Welsh Surnames* (Cardiff,1985).
WWW.   Gwyn A. Williams, *When Was Wales?* (London, 1991[1985]).
YEE.   Bedwyr Lewis Jones, *Yn Ei Elfen* (Llanrwst,1992).

The village evolved as a result of this and other industrial developments. *Aberaman House* was later to become the headquarters of the Powell Duffryn Co.

Treaman, 1851, the name of a colliery (also known as *Nicky Nocky*, apparently because of the noise of the machinery) and the railway station (renamed *Aberaman*, 1889), did not survive as the name of the settlement.

The name *Aberaman*, refers to the place where the river Aman flows into the river *Cynon*.

pron. ah-berr <u>am</u> an. aber<u>am</u>an.[stress underlined consonant].

Sp. Aberaman.

Literal meaning:- Mouth of the river Aman.

ABERCYNON

Abercynon.   *1893.*   *SoA. 9.*
Abercynon Colliery. *1896.*   *MAP&A.19.*
Abercynon.   *1896.*   *PNG.HCJ.*
Abercynon   *1908.   Abercynon was formerly known as Navigation, (first terminus of the canal) CFE/SG 59. PNC,Bangor.*

Welsh 'Aber' + 'Cynon'.

Aber = the mouth of a river. (see Aberaman).

Cynon = river name.

There have been many attempts to explain the meaning of the river-name *Cynon*. Here are two of the most feasible.
1. *Cynon*, (Canan 1253, Kenon 1536-9, Kynon 1638) may represent the name of the 'hound-goddess'. RJT. MR. BFR.
2. *Cynon* is a river named after a person. cf. *Alun, Dewi, Meurig, Pedran, Beuno, Cynfael, Einion, Machno*, etc. (There are many examples of Welsh pers. name *Cynon*.

eg. *Cynon* ap Brychan; *Cynon* Sant, linked with Tregynon, Powys; *Cynon* ap Ceredig, etc).

The village takes its name from the place where the river *Cynon* joins the river *Taf*. *Abercynon* became the settlement name at the end of the 19th.cent. Prior to *Abercynon* other names were used for parts of the settlement:-

Abertaffacynon (1813/14 OSM) a farm name, means the joining place of the *Taf* and *Cynon* rivers. 'The 1670 form of '*Tavern Kennon hamlett* in Merthir Tidvill parich' on p139 is later given as *Taff and Cynon hamlet*, p.lxvi.' (TE). It would seem probable that 'Tavern' is an attempt at '*Tav an' Cynon'* for *Taf and Cynon.*

Y Basin (c1850), means the basin and refers to the part of the canal at *Abertaff a Cynon* that had been widened in order to become a landing place for the loading and unloading of boats, barges etc.

Navigation and *Navigation House (1830),* are also names linked with the canal era, *navigation* being another name for a canal. In this case, it was the *Glamorgan Canal*, linking Merthyr Tydfil and Cardiff. It opened in 1792 and closed c1900 (see CWV). The *Aberdare Canal* [opened 1812, closed 1900, (OA.vol.6.)] joined the *Glamorgan Canal* just above the aquaduct that carried the *Glamorgan Canal* over the river *Taff* at *Abertaff and Cynon.* [see 1842 Tithe Map].

(*navvies* were originally *navigators* working on *navigations*, ie. canal building labourers employed in the construction of canals; the word extended later to those who dug the foundations and tunnels for the railways).

In 1840, the Taff Vale Railway Station was opened here and was known as *Navigation House*, but in 1846 this was changed to *Aberdare Junction.* cf. *Junction Hotel*, Station Road.

In 1896 the station and village officially became known as *Abercynon.* (TE, SoA. village assumed name in 1893).

pron. ah berr <u>kun</u>-non. aber<u>cyn</u>on

Sp. Abercynon.

Literal meaning:- Mouth of the river Cynon.

ABERNANT-Y-WENALLT

Tyr Aber Nant y Wenallte.	*1632.*	*SAPN. 7.*
gwayn nant y wenallt.	*17th cent.RR.Meisg.437.*	
Abernant y Wenallt.	*17th cent.RR. ibid.*	
Abernant y Wenathl.	*1778. SAPN. 7.(note orthography of*	
'll').		
Blaen-y-Wenallt.	*1799.*	*George Yates's map.*
Abernant y Wenallt	*1801, leased to Jeremiah Homfray &*	
James Birch of Abernant.CVAI.20.		
Abernant Iron Company.	*1802.*	*CVAI. 21.*
Abernant Iron Company.	*1804.*	*APP.46.*
Abernant.	*1806.*	*GRO. MR. PNC,Bangor.*
Abernant Furnace.	*1814.*	*OS map.*
Nantywenallt.	*1814.*	*OS map.*
Abernant House.	*1832.*	*Dawson's Map. APP. 2.*
Abernant.	*1833.*	*OS. MR.PNC,Bangor.*
Nant y Wenallt.	*1833.*	*OS1". reprint 1980.*
Abernant Station,VN Rlway,	*c1870.*	*OS1". reprint 1980.*
Abernant Place, Abernant Row	*.c1890.*	*APP.2.154.*

Welsh.   Aber + nant + y + gwenallt.

Aber = mouth of river or stream.

Nant = a stream.   y = the.

Gwenallt (white wooded slope) = stream-name.

Gwenallt or *Y Wenallt* is the Welsh equivalent of the poetical English 'milk wood'.
[*Dan y Wenallt* is the Welsh translation for Dylan Thomas's *Under Milk Wood*] and it is likely that the stream derived its name as it flowed through such a wood i.e. 'the milk wood stream'.
> NB. *Gwenallt* is actually a composite word of 'gwen', feminine form of 'gwyn' (white) and 'allt' (wooded hillside) and literally means white wooded slope/hill. (The same elements are to be found in a different order in *Alltwen* near Pontardawe).

cf. *Blaen-y-Wenallt.* 1799. GY. which means the head or source of the Wenallt (stream), the street name *Wenallt Road* and public house *The Rhos Wenallt (1895)* (moorland of the Wenallt).

Abernant derives its name from the place where the *Nant-y-Wenallt* joins the river Cynon.

This became the name of a nearby farm, and in turn gave its name to *Abernant House* (site of today's Aberdare Hospital), the home of the ironmasters who built *Abernant Iron Works* (1804); Note that the name *Pentrebach* [little village] appears on the 1814 OS map; the Vale of Neath Railway company constructed *Abernant Station* c1853, the final station before entering the tunnel on the Neath-Merthyr railway line [previous Cynon Valley stops on this line were at *Rhigos Halt, Hirwaun* and *Llwydcoed*].

The name became that of the village, the road leading to the village, as well as the name of two rows of terraced houses on the banks of the *Cynon*.

The name *Abernant-y-wenallt*, originally the name of the confluence (you can see it just above the Trap bridge) lent itself to the farm-name *Tir Abernant-y-wenallt*, was used in its contracted form for the *Abernant Iron Company, Abernant Furnace, Abernant House* [built by James Birch, 1804, on the site of Cynnon Farm (TE.)], *Abernant railway station* and *Abernant village*, all quite a distance from the confluence of the *Nant-y-wenallt* stream with the river Cynon.

The movement of a name such as *Abernant* from the original river mouth location to adjoining areas is not uncommon in place-names.

pron. ah berr nant ugh <u>wen</u> aah-llt ('ll' as in Llanelli). abernant-y-<u>wen</u>allt.

Sp. Abernant-y-wenallt.

Literal meaning:- Mouth of the Wenallt stream.

ABERDÂR   ABERDARE

Aberdar.	1203.	MR.NTCB 29.
Aberdare.	1203	Margam.174.RJT.Meisg.60.
Aberdare.	1253	Margam.267.RJT.Meisg.60.
Aberdaer.	1348	MR.NTCB 29.
Aber Dar.	15th cent.	Lewis Glyn Cothi.RJT.Meisg.60.
Aberdare.	1528-33	Cart.Glam.V.1853.RJT.Meisg.60.

Aberdayer.	*1536-9*	*Itin.Leland.RJT.Meisg.60.*
Abr(sic) Daer.	*1559*	*Card.Recs.iv.84.RJT.Meisg.60.*
Aberdaer.	*1578*	*Glam.Ants.110.RJT.Meisg.60.*
Aberdaer.	*1585*	*Dafydd Benwyn.RJT.Meisg.60.*
Aberdare.	*1610*	*Speede.RJT.Meisg.60.*
Aberdare.	*1622-3*	*Plymouth.MR. PNC,Bangor.*
Aberdaer.	*1626*	*Tredegar.PNC,Bangor.*
Aberdar.	*1699*	*Lhuyd.Paroch.iii.7.RJT.Meisg.60.*
Aberdare.	*1699*	*Lhuyd.Paroch.iii.7.RJT.Meisg.60.*
Aberdaer.	*1729*	*Bowen.RJT.Meisg.60.*
Aberdare.	*1799*	*Yates.RJT.Meisg.60.*
Aberdare.	*1833*	*Colby.RJT.Meisg.60.*
Aberdare.	*1844*	*TS.*

Welsh.   Aber + Dâr (e)

Aber = Mouth of river or stream

It would appear that the etymology of the second element 'dâr' is uncertain, with 'dâr' (wild) and 'dyar' (noise) being considered, while I am inclined to favour 'dâr' linked with oak trees. ie. a river that flows through oak woods, as it fits in with the Brythonic/Celtic pattern of linking the names of rivers with their woodland environment, eg.
Derwennydd, (Wales), *Daren, Dart, Darwen, Derwent,* (Eng.),
Derrylough, Derravarragh (Ire.) are all related to rivers or lakes where oaks were common.
Examples of river-names in Wales linked to other species of trees are :
Celynen (holly), *Cerdinen* (Rowan), *Helygen*, (willow) and
Llwyfen, (elm).
In England, the following are Brythonic/Celtic river-names linked with trees:
Warren, (alders, cf. Welsh, gwern.) *Cole*, (hazel, cf. Welsh, collen) and
Leam, Lemon, Lymn, (elm, cf. Welsh, llwyfen).
It must also be remembered that in the reign of Elizabeth the first, the Cynon valley was renowned for its fine woodland. cf. Anon. 16th century poem 'Coed Glyn Cynon' (the woods of the Cynon valley).
Examples of place-names in the Cynon valley linked with trees are:-
Nant-y-Wenallt (milk-wood), *Llwydcoed* (grey woods), *Pant-y-Gerdinen,* (rowan), *Mountain Ash, Llwyn Onn* (ash), *Llwyn Celyn, Perthcelyn,* (holly), *Fedw Hir, Tyle'r fedw,* (birch), *Nant-yr-Afallen,* (apple), *Llwyn helyg* (willow) etc.

Oak trees and rivers were important elements in ancient Celtic religion. cf. *Daron* the Welsh goddess of the oaks and *Dervonae* her French Celtic counterpart. Oak trees are still numerous in this area.

The *Cambrian Traveller's Guide*, published in 1813, describes the village of Aberdare where on the banks of the river Cynon there is "a most luxuriant and majestic grove of oak". *Aberdare Leader*, Jan.1997. There is much circumstantial evidence therefore to support the 'river of the oak woodlands' theory. On the other hand, it is quite feasible that the second element *dar* is 'anger, tumult, noise'.

pron. ah berr dair (with rolled 'r'). aber<u>dare</u>.

NB.the local dialect pronounciation of Welsh 'a' is as Welsh 'e'. In this dialect, Aber<u>dar</u> would sound as Aber<u>der</u> or 'Ber<u>der</u>. This is much the same sound as the present local pron. Aberdare, but with pronounced and rolled 'r's.

Sp.   Aberdâr. Aberdare.

Literal meaning:- Mouth of the river Dâr.(Dare).

ABERPENNAR   MOUNTAIN ASH

Aber Pennarthe	1570.	*G.S.RJT.Meisg.63.*
Aber Penarth	1638.	*CFL Glm. MR.PNC,Bangor.*
Tir Aber-Penarth	1666.	*M.M. RJT.Meisg.63.*
Aberpennarth	*17ganrif,*	*M.C. (Cymr)RJT.Meisg.63.*
Aberpennar alias Dyffryn	1691.	*GP.WM.*
Dyffrin alias Aberpennar	1717.	*GP.WM.*
Tyr Aberpennar	*1771-81,*	*S.R.RJT.Meisg.63.*
Duffrin Aberdaer	1799.	*Yates's map.CVAI.14.*
Mountain Ash (Inn)	1809.	*HCJ.PNG.29.*
Mountain Ash	1814.	*OS.Aberdare Library.*
Mountain Ash Pub.Hse	1844.	*TS.[Abercwmboi Isaf.]*
Mountain Ash Cres.	*1842-50.*	*9 houses.HMH.112-4.*
Mountain Ash Inn	1852.	*GP.WM.*
Mountain Ash Station	*c 1860.*	*OSM1" 1833.reprint.1980.*
Aberpenar	1874.	*Hanes Morg,429.RJT.Meisg.63.*
Aberpennar.Mountain Ash	*1905.RNEW programme cover.MAP&A .*	
Mountain Ash (Aberpennar)	1989.	*OS Pathfinder 1129.*

24

English   Mountain Ash. Name of the rowan tree given to an inn.

Welsh   Aber + pennar.

Aber = mouth or confluence of river or stream.

Pennar = name of stream.

RJT. states that *Penar* in *Aberpenar (th)* was so called from the name of its source. ie. pen (top of) & ardd (height, headland, hill, ridge.)
MR.& GP. agree that the brook takes its name from the mountain where it rises, ie. *pennar(dd)* which means a promontory, ridge or mountain height. cf. *Cwmpennar* and *Cefnpennar*.
The land of *Aberpennar* was chosen for the site of *Dyffryn House* (pre.1699) later, the home of the Bruce family. (Note the prior alias names of 1691 & 1717.) see *Dyffryn*.
BFR informs me that R.T.Jenkins writing in an *Aberpennar National Eisteddfod* publication of 1940 states (and I translate): 'What is the Welsh name for *Mountain Ash*? Well, there wasn't one. It would appear that somebody thought that *Mountain Ash* would do for *Pont-mynydd-y-gerdinen* [the rowan-mountain bridge] but that *rowan* (mountain ash) would have been on the mountain and not by the bridge.
What about *Aberpennar*?
It will do splendidly, and we will steadfastly adhere to it, but let us not be led to believe that it was the first name of the town - it would seem that the old name *Plas y Dyffryn* (Dyffryn House/mansion) has that distinction.'
Mountain Ash was the name given to a public house, (on the other side of the river *Cynon* to *Dyffryn*) reputedly in 1809, by the wife of landowner and industrialist John Bruce Price, because of the presence of Rowan trees or saplings on the proposed building site. It appears as *Mountain Ash* on the 1814 OS map and as the *Mountain Ash Public House,* under *Abercwmboi Isaf* on the 1844 Tithe Schedules. *The Mountain Ash Inn* today stands in Commercial Street.
Both the Welsh and English names were used for the town in 1905 when the National Eisteddfod of Wales visited the area.
Incidentally the Welsh name for the *Rowan* tree or *Mountain Ash* is *Cerddinen* or *Cerdinen* (both are found). cf. *Pant-y-Gerddinen, Gerdinen terrace* and *Pant-y-Cerdin* (Cwmbach).

Aberpennar takes its name from the place where the *Pennar* stream joins the river *Cynon*.

25

pron. ah berr penarr. aberpennar.

SP. *Aberpennar.*
Literal meaning:- Mouth of the Pennar stream,

Mountain Ash.
Literal Meaning:- the Rowan tree.

ABERCWMBOI   ABERCWM-BOI

Ab' Ken' Voye	1547.	*Card.Recs.1.247.RJT.Meisg.63.*
Ab Ken voye	1550.	*Cal Pat R.MR.PNC,Bangor.*
Abkon-voye	1551.	*Card.Recs.1.464.RJT.Meisg.63.*
Aber Convoye Yssa	1570.	*G.S.RJT.Meisg.63.*
Aber Convoy Ycha,		
Aber Convoy Yssa	1638.	*CFL.gem.MR.Pnc,Bangor.*
Aber Convoy	1666.	*M.M.RJT.Meisg.63.*
Aber Convoy Isha	*17th cent.M.C.RJT.Meisc.63.*	
Abercwmvoy	1720.	*SAPN.7.*
Aberconvey	1771.	*SAPN.7.*
Abercwmfoi Issa	1788.	*S.R.1788.RJT.Meisg.63.*
Abercwmboy	1798.	*Senghennydd.MR.Pnc,Bangor.*
Abercwmboi	1807.	*PR.Aberdare Library.*
Abercwmboy	1814.	*OS map.Aberdare Library.*
Abercwmboi isaf &		
Abercwmboy Farm	1844.	*TS.Aberdare.*
Abercwmboi	1989.	*Landranger.170.*
Abercwmboi	1989.	*GWPN.*

There are differences in the recording of the second element (*Cynfoi >
Cwmboi*) which make it difficult to ascertain the true etymology of the
place name. All the early forms from 1570, record *Kenvoy* or *convoy*.
The form *cwmboy* does not appear until 1798.
It is possible that the earlier form *Convoy* is Goidelic (from which Irish
Gaelic, Manx and Scots Gaelic are descended). Coincidentally there is a
Convoy place-name in Ireland meaning 'hound plain'. Other examples of
place-names in the Cynon valley containing Goidelic elements are :-
Clydach (Ir. Cleidach,Cloidach, meaning a stream with a stony bed *);
Clun gwyn (Ir. cluain,* meaning pasture*); Esgair-y-llaethdy (Ir. eiscir,*
meaning a ridge) etc.

On the other hand, it is possible that *Convoy* is Brythonic (from which Welsh, Cornish and Breton are descended) or Welsh, *Cynfoi*. It would seem that *Cwmboi* has resulted through a process of assimilation [nf -> mf -> mb] and is an attempt at rationalising the previous *Cynvoi*. Both would be pronounced with the emphasis on the final syllable, as is the case of all mono-syllabic words following cwm. eg. *Cwm-bach, Cwm-twrch, Cwm-nedd, Cwm-dâr, Cwm-parc,* etc.

Aber = mouth of river or stream.

Cwmboi = local rationalisation of *Cynfoi*

MR suggests that *Cynvoe* is a pers. name, and the stream could take its name from the person, ie. *Cynvoe stream*. The pers. name appears in the forms *Convoe* and *Convoi* in the *Book of Llandav* c1150. (GOP, WM). The naming of a stream or river after a person is not uncommon, see *Abercynon*.
In its present form we can interprate the meaning as the mouth of the stream *Cwmboi,* from an earlier name meaning *Cynfoi's stream/Cynfoi stream*. (aber can also mean stream).

The village is sometimes called *Cap Coch.*
'Llewelyn in his first essay of Gardd Aberdar [1854] mentions the legend then current that *Cap Coch* derived its name for a local publican from the early 17th century who wore a red cap on cockfighting occasions. This is not the present *Cap Coch public house* which dates from 1865, ie. 11 years after Llewelyn's essay.' TE.
Cap Coch is also the name of the village primary school.

PS. signs of early habitation.
   Bronze-age socketed axe head found in Abercwmboi in
   1898.
pron. ah berr koom <u>boee.</u>   abercwm<u>boi.</u>

Sp. Abercwmboi.

Lit. meaning:- Confluence of the stream Cwmboi [from earlier 'Cynfoi'].

ABER-FFRWD

aberfrood	*1594*	*SAPN.7.*	
tir aberffrwd.	*1666*	*ibid.*	
Tir Aberffrwd	*17th.cent.*	*Meisg.437.*	
Aberffrwd	*1814*	*OS*	*Aberdare Library.*
Aberffurd	*1841*	*Cens.*	*ibid.*
Aberffrwd	*1842-50*	*PRB.*	*HMH.109.*
Aberfrwd	*1844*	*TS.Aberdare.*	
Aberffrwd cemtry	*1863-5*	*HMH.91.*	
Aberffrwd	*1875*	*OS.*	*Aberdare Library.*
Aberffrwd Road	*1995*	*MSP.*	

Welsh   'aber' + 'ffrwd'.

aber   =   river mouth; confluence.

ffrwd = 'swift stream, torrent, flood, current'. GPC.
           'stream'. GM. 'brook'. RJT. EANC. 67.

Often *ffrwd*, a general name for a brook, becomes the actual name of the brook.
cf. *Avon*, generally meaning 'a river', (Brit, *abona; Welsh 'afon') is an actual river-name for four English rivers. The original river names which would have followed *avon*, are lost. [cf. in Wales, *Afon Dâr; Afon Cynon; Afon Aman; Afon Taf,* etc.]

also cf. *Y Ffrwd, Llanwynno* and *Glanffrwd,* [the poet].*

*It has often been the case in Wales for local poets to adopt the name of their village, farm etc (or a form of the name) as their literary name. e.g. the poet *Glanffrwd*, William Thomas 1843 - 90.
cf.   William Williams, *Pantycelyn* (farm); *Gwenallt*, David Gwenallt Jones from Alltwen (village), Pontardawe; John Jenkins, *Gwili* (river); John Hughes, *Ceiriog* (river); David Thomas, *Dafydd Ddu Eryri* (mountain range); Evan Rees, *Dyfed* (territory); Thomas Evans, *Tomos Glyn Cothi* (valley); Richard Parry, *Gwalchmai* (village); Rowland Williams, *Hwfa Môn* (island); etc.

pron. ah berr ffroode [rhymes with Eng. food].

Sp. Aber-ffrwd.

Lit.meaning:- brook confluence.

ABER-GWAWR

Aber Gwaynee	*1570*	*G.S.(sic).*	*Meisg.63.*
[cf.Blayne gwawr	*1592*	*SAPN].*	
tyr abergwawr	*1632*	*SAPN.*	
Tyre Abergwawre	*1638*	*S.M.1638*	*Meisg.63.*
Tir Abergwawr	*1666*	*M.M.*	*ibid.*
Abergwair	*1799*	*Yates.*	*CVAI.14.*
Abergwawr	*1814*	*OS.*	*Aberdare Library.*
Abergwawr	*1844*	*TS.Aberdare.*	
Abergwawr Collier	*1854*	*APP.vol.1.57.*	
Abergwawr House	*1919*	*OS.*	
Abergwawr Colliery	*1919*	*ibid.*	
Abergwawr St	*1995*	*MSP.*	

Welsh   'aber'   +   'Gwawr'.

aber   =   river mouth; confluence.

Gwawr   =   river name. see Blaengwawr.

Aber Gwaynee, 1570 obviously has a spelling error ('n' for 'r'), note Yates's *Abergwair* of 1799.   *Abergwair* itself is an attempt by an Englishman at writing the *gwawr* sound which does not occur in the English language (see pron.).

Tir Abergwawr refers to the farmstead (lit. the land) of *Abergwawr.*

BFR informs me that 'tir' literally meaning land is often used in place-names with a meaning of a farm or farmstead, ie. land with a house and other buildings.

eg. *Tir Dafydd Sais* (David the English speaker or Englishman), Aberdare; *Tir Evan y Gof* (the smith), Aberdare; *Tir Ioryn* (pet form of Iorwerth), Aberdare, etc.

cf. the use of 'cae' in some parts of Wales, especially when followed by a person's name or occupation,

eg. *Caeathro*, Gwynedd; *Caeharris*, Merthyr Tydfil; *Cae cashier*, Aberdare; *Cae Jacky,* Aberdare; *Cae Luce,* Aberdare etc.

The *Abergwawr* name was later adopted by the colliery and it remains with us today as *Abergwawr Street*.

pron.   ah-berr <u>gwah-oo</u>re [as in chi<u>huahua</u>.]

Sp. Aber-gwawr.

Lit.meaning:- confluence (of the) Gwawr (stream).

BLAEN-NANT-Y-GROES

Blaennant-y-groes	*1582*	*SAPN.8.*
Blaennant-y-groes	*1600*	*ibid.*
Blaenant-y-groes	*1606*	*ibid.*
Blaen Nant y Groes	*1841*	*cens.Library.*
Blaen Nanty Groes	*1844*	*TM.Aberdare.*
Blaenant y groes	*1844*	*TS.Aberdare.*
Blaen-nant-y-groes	*1919*	*OS.25".*
Blaennantygroes	*1995*	*MSP.Aberdare.*

Welsh   'blaen' + 'nant' + 'y' + 'croes'.
blaen   =   upper reaches, source. (see Blaengwawr).
nant   =   "originally' valley, ravine, glen', later developing the sense 'stream, rivulet, brook etc'". GP. PNDPH. 345.
y   =   the
croes   =   1. a cross, used for crucifiction;
             2. emblem of Christianity; crucifix;
             3. monument or other structure in the
                form of a cross; wooden or stone cross.
             4. crossroads.

Nant-y-groes is the name of the stream that flows from *Blaen-nant-y-groes* to its confluence with the Cynon at *Abernant-y-groes*.

The three farmsteads with lands adjoining the stream took their names from the stream, ie. *Abernant y Groes Isaf,* (Groes stream confluence lower farm) *Abernant y Groes Uchaf (Gro*es stream confluence higher farm) and *Blaen-nant y Groes* (source of the Groes stream).

Some local people refer to the settlement at *Blaen-nant-y-groes* as the

Tunnel, due to its proximity to the disused Merthyr (railway) Tunnel and to the disused Tunnel (coal) Pit. [see OS.1919]. Telynog wrote a verse about the railway tunnel c1860 called 'Y Tunnel' :-

"FFORDD dywell, hen gell ddu gau, – yw Tunnel
  O tan y mynyddau;
Pur hynod, rhed Peiriannau
Drwyddo ar hynt, fel gwynt yn gwau."

A dark road, an old false black cell, – is a tunnel
  under the mountains;
truly remarkable, engines run through it on a journey,
like weaving wind.

The stream *Nant-y-groes* probably takes its name from a boundary marker or monument at its source or on its banks, originally in the shape of a cross, prob. religious.
A 7th-9th cent. cross-incised pillar stone was found in 1925 at *Panwaun pwll-gwellt, Mynydd Merthyr*, just west of the *Llanwynno* parish boundary. I am grateful to Dr Mark Redknap of the National Museum of Wales for this information. The pillar is on display at the National Museum of Wales.

It is quite possible that there was a similar stone cross linked to the *Nant-y-groes* stream, thereby giving it its name. As Dr Redknap explains:-"So many stones have disappeared through the centuries, many eventually being rediscovered in field boundaries and walls."

cf. *Cae Cristinas* (Christian or poss. Christina's field) *Abernant-y-groes Uchaf* TS. 888; & *Ty Llwyd* (poss. Holy House) the name of the neighbouring farm to *Abernant-y-groes Isha*. TM. 1844; also *Bôn-y-groes* (the base, stump of the cross), Aberdare, name for a public house, closed 1827, situated on the site of the old *Market House*. The name relates to the ancient custom of erecting a cross near the gates of the parish church, which were nearby.

Circumstantial evidence would stongly support the association of the stream-name *Nant-y-groes* with an early Christian cross, probably of stone, or engraved on a stone pillar.

The local dial. pron. is *Blan*-nant-y-g*ros*. {seeMeisg. 17. & Yates map, 1799, *Abernant y Grose*).

pron. blah-een nant ugh gro-ice. Blaen-nant-y-<u>groes.</u>

local dial. pron. blan-nant y gros.

Sp. Blaen-nant-y-groes.

Lit. meaning:- source (of the) stream of the cross.

BLAEN-GWAWR

blayne gwawr	*1592*	*SAPN.7.*	
Blaengwawa	*1814*	*OS.*	*Aberdare Library.*
Blaengwawr	*1833*	*OS.*	*PNCB.*
Blaengwawr	*1844*	*TM.Aberdare.*	
Blaengwawr	*1853*	*Senghennydd.*	*MR.PNCB.*
Blaengwawr Inn	*1855*	*IHBHAD.sn.*	
Blaengwawr Comp.Sch.	*1995*	*CVOH.31.*	

Welsh 'blaen' + river name 'Gwawr'.

blaen = headwater; source of a river stream or brook;
$\qquad\qquad\qquad$ head of a valley.
Gwawr = name of brook.

The first element *blaen* in *Blaengwawr* is common in many Welsh place-names and refers to the source of a river or stream, at the very top end of a valley.
eg. *Blaenrhondda, Blaenafon, Blaendulais* etc. *Blaenau* is the plural form meaning an area with a number of river sources, or valley heads, i.e. uplands. cf. *Blaenau Gwent* (the valley heads of Gwent), *Blaenau Ffestiniog* (valley heads of land of Ffestin) and *Blaenau'r Dyffrynoedd* (Heads of the Valleys).

The second element *gwawr* is the name of the brook. There is a Welsh word *gwawr* meaning 'dawn' ie. the break of day. JM suggests that the river is so named as it faces east and therefore greets the dawn.

GBGG links the name of the brook to the personal name 'Gwawr ferch Frychan' (Gwawr the daughter of Brychan).

gwawr can also mean princess, lady, maiden.see GPC.

Other place-names linked with Brychan (5th century chieftain) and his offspring are:-

Brycheiniog (the land of *Brychan*, cf. Breconshire);

Merthyr Tydfil (*Tudful* was a daughter);

Hafod Tanglwyst near Aberfan (*Tanglwystl* was a daughter);

Cilsanws near Cefn Coed (*Sanos* was a daughter);

Dol Gynog (Penderyn), *Merthyr Cynog, Llangynog* (*Cynog* was a son).etc.

Blaengwawr is now the name of a town district, an electoral ward, a Comprehensive School and a Public House. *Rhos Gwawr* is further up the hillside and means the moorland of the *Gwawr* brook.

BFR suggests it may be possible that *Rhos Gwawr* is the primary name and that the stream took its name from its source. ie. *Nant (Rhos) Gwawr.* cf. *Pennar.*

pron. blah-een goo-aah-oor. see Abergwawr. blae<u>ngwawr.</u>

Sp. Blaen-gwawr.

Literal meaning:- Headwater of the Gwawr (brook).

BODWIGIAD

Bodwigiad	*1622*	*Hbiv,* 72.	*PNDH.*
Bodwigad	*1729*	*Emanuel Bowen's map of South Wales*	
Bodwicced	*1748*	*WP.* *PNDH.*	
Bodwigad	*1765*	*Kitchen ibid.*	
Bodwiggied	*1785*	*HBiv. 64. ibid.*	
Bodwigad		(*corrupted from*)*Bodwaun-y-Gad 1833.TDII,309,1809*	
HBiv,65. ibid.			
Bodwiggiad	*1840*	*TM. 1830 OS. ibid.*	
Bodwigiad Arms	*1906*	*OS6".* .	
Bodwigiad	*1905*	*HPP. 14, 1841-81 Cens.*	

Welsh   'bod'   +   difficult second element, poss.
          'ewigiaid', or pers.name 'Gwigiad'.

bod = permanent home, abode, dwelling, residence. (GPC).

wigiad =   1. poss. derived from *ewigiaid*, (Eng. hinds, female deer). TR.
2. poss. pers. name *Gwigiad*.

Name of old mansion, farmhouse and lodge in *Penderyn*.
Public House *The Bodwigiad Arms,* Hirwaun.

Bod is a fairly common element in Welsh place-names, but it is rarely to be found in the south. Apparently it appears in *Bodlwynog* (known today as Bedlinog) *Bodfelltau* (known today as Bedwellty) *Crookebotruan* (crug + bod + Rhufawn = *mound of Rhufawn's abode [Rhufawn = Lat. Romanus] see Meisg.156*) and *Bodwigiad*. There are more *bod* place-names in Anglesey than any other Welsh district.

The second element *wigiad* poses a problem. Although it is relatively consistent in recorded forms (apart from the erroneous Bodwaun-y-gad) it is not recognisable in this form. It seems there are two etymological possibilities.
1. TR. suggests it is derived from *ewigiaid*, 'hinds, female deer' and there are examples of *bod* names followed by an animal element. eg. *Bodychen* (ox), *Bodwylan* (gwylan = sea-gull), *Bodlew* (poss.lion).
The plural suffix *iaid* is connected with animals.(TR.)
eg. *anifeiliaid* (animals); *bleiddiaid* (wolves); *creaduriaid* (creatures); *ewigiaid* etc.
It is possible that the name evolved because it was an area frequented by hinds or possibly a place for hunting deer. Deer hunting used to be a popular activity with the gentry. cf. Pwyll Pendefig Dyfed's meeting with Arawn in PKM.
2. It could also, more probably, be the pers. name *Gwigiad*. see GBGG. Many *bod* place-names are followed by pers. names,
eg. Bodangharad (*Angharad*), Bodfeurig (*Meurig*),
  Bodgadfedd (*Cadfedd*), Bodgadfan (*Cadfan*),
  Bodidris (*Idris*), Bodiddan (*Iddan*), Boteiniol (*Deiniol*),
  Botegwal (*Tegwal*), Bodwion (*Gwion*), etc.
In the seventeenth century, (1620-47) *Bodwigiad,* a manor house was occupied by Richard Games, a very powerful Breconshire JP and High Sheriff. (see *Penderyn, a History* by Nansi Selwood.)
The name survives as a farm name and as *The Bodwigiad Arms,* Hirwaun.

pron. bode wigg ee-ad. bod<u>w</u>igiad

Sp. Bodwigiad.

Literal meaning:- 1. dwelling place where hinds are common.
           or
           2. Gwigiad's residence.

BWLCH-Y-LLADRON (lost) and CRAIG-Y-BWLCH

Bwlch y lladron	*1666*	*SAPN.8.*
Bulch Lladron	*1729*	*E.Bowen map of s.Wales.*
Bwlch-y-lladron	*1830*	*OSM.*
Bwlch-lled-y-rhiw	*1854*	*GA.*
Craig-y-bwlch	*1954*	*OSM.*

Welsh   'bwlch' + 'lladron'.

'bwlch' = 'gap, pass, mountain pass, defile, passage'.

'y' = def. article. (Eng. 'the').

'lladron' = plural form of 'lleidr', 'thief, robber, bandit, snatcher, depredator, plunderer; malefactor, evil-doer, criminal'. GPC.
cf. Pant-y-*lladron*, Llantriddyd. PNDPH, 128.
This is an example of a place-name changing in order to gain respectability. For hundreds of years it had been *Bwlch-y-lladron* (the bandits' mountain pass) but in 1854, possibly as the result of the 'Treason of the Blue Books' (1847) or because of prim Victorian values, or possibly both, the name was changed to the clumsy *Bwlch-lled-y-rhiw* (the pass of the width of the hill). This was not uncommon in Victorian Wales.
eg. Cwmrhyd-y-*ceirw* < Cwmrhyd-y-*cwrw* (beer);
    Ffynon *Groyw*   < Ffynnon y *cwrw* (beer);
    Pont-y-*Clun* < Pont-y-*clown*;   *Cadole* < *Catshole*;
    Pandy *Tudur* < Pandy *Budr* (dirty); etc.
Craig-y-bwlch (the mountain pass rock) could poss. be an abbreviation of *Craig bwlch-y-lladron*, as it is situated just above the pass.

pron. Krah-eegg ugh boolch(guttral). craig y <u>bwlch</u>.

pron. bool-ch(guttral) ugh llad-ron. bwlchy<u>lla</u>dron.('ll' as in Llanelli).

Sp. Bwlch-y-lladron.

Literal meaning:- The bandits' mountain pass.

BWLLFA DÂR   BWLLFA DARE

Puthladar	*1253*	*Margam 267. Meisg.68.*
Pulthadar	*1256*	*Cart.Glam.II.615. ibid.*
Pulla Dare	*1570*	*G.S. ibid.*
y Bwllva	*17th.cent. Meisg.436.*	
Byllfa	*1739*	*PR.Aberdare Library.*
Tyr y Pwllva Ddare	*1771-81*	*S.R. Meisg.68.*
Bwllva	*1804*	*PR.Aberdare Library.*
Bwllfaddar	*1809-36*	*O.S.M.1809-36.ibid.*
Bwllfa	*1844*	*TM.Aberdare.*
Byllfa Dda	*1854*	*SAPN.8.*
Bwllfa Dare Colliery	*1856*	*APP.1. 64.*

Welsh   'pwllfa' + 'Dâr', 'Dare', river name.

"'Pwllfa' is a hollow, gorge, basin, often at the source of a river or stream and occurs as a place-name element in the heads of the Glamorgan valleys and parts of Carmarthenshire." (RJT.Meisg. 46. trans.)
eg. *Bwllfa*, Penderyn (PNDH.7.11.), *Bwllfa* Aman, (SAPN. 8), *Bwllfa*-foel, (ibid), Craig-y-*Bwllfa*, (OSM, Pathfinder1108), Mynydd *Bwllfa* (ibid), etc.

Prior to the 1850s, *Bwllfa* or *Pwllfa Dare* was a farmstead or small-holding. However, in the early 1850s a colliery was sunk by Samuel Thomas and Thomas Joseph, so that in 1856 the *Bwllfa Dare Colliery* started producing coal, and a small settlement developed around the colliery. The name *pwllfa* however is far, far older than that of the colliery, although it is sometimes erroneously considered to mean a coal pit, possibly because of its similarity to *pwll glo* (coal pit).

For *Dâr/Dare*, river name, see Aberdare.
It is interesting to note the attempt by 13th century scribes at reproducing the 'll' sound. see *Puthladar* and *Pulthadar* above. Cf. Shakespeare's *Fluellen*.

pron. boollva ('ll' as in Llanelli) dare. bwllfa dare.

Sp. Bwllfa Dâr/Dare.

Literal meaning:- Hollow at the source of the river Dare.

CAE FELIN PARC   PARC CAE'R FELIN

Coed car felin	*1800*	*PNDH.7.27.2.*
Coedcae Melin y Rhydiau	*1802*	*ibid.7.27.3.*
Coedcaefellin	*1813*	*ibid.7.27.2.*
Mill Cottage,Maes y Rhydia	*1841*	*TS.Penderyn*
Coedcaeyrfelin	*1879*	*PNDH.7.27.2.*
Coedcaefelin Farm	*1905*	*ibid.*
Coedcae'rfelin	*1905*	*HPP.17.*
Cae Felin Parc	*1994*	*CVOH.39.*

Welsh   'cae' + 'melin' + 'parc'.

cae = a field.

melin = a mill.

parc = Eng. 'park', name used with modern housing
                development.

The mill indicated in the earlier place-names is the mill on *Maes y Rhydiau* (field of the fords) Farm. [Note the 1802 & 1841 forms].
"On this Coedcae (Coedcae'r felin) stood 'Yr Hen Felin' (the old mill) Melin y Rhydiau (Mill of the fords);......" HPP.17.
Coedcae is often found as an element in Welsh place-names. Hywel Wyn Owen, writing in *Ditectif Geiriau*, Western Mail, says that the original *coedcae* was a type of quick-set hedge. Then it was used for a place that was enclosed by such a hedge. Later, within the last three hundred years, nearly every *coedcae* was on relatively high land, with the hedge that enclosed it securing some pasture in the rough and wild mountain land.
R.F.Peter Powell in PNDH 7.26. adds that in this locality (Hirwaun) many of the fields have stone walls and have never had hedges. He also submits that in this locality the place-name element *coedcae* has the

meaning of rough grazing land or simply scrubland. (also see Llwydcoed, 47, for RJT's definition and 'Coedcae as a Welsh Place-name' by W.Linnard, Studia Celtica XVI-XVII,183).

The present estate was built during the 1970-80s and takes its name from the earlier *Coedcae'r felin*, in the abbreviated form *Cae'r felin* plus the ubiquitous park, parc.

'*Coed car felin* is probably dialect form of *coedcae'r felin,* cf. 1813, 1879, 1905.
Cae Felin - really needs '**r** to explain the mutation of m > f.
Parc Cae'r Felin is a far better Welsh form and should be encouraged'. BFR.

pron. kah-ee velin park. park(short 'a') kah-eer velin.

Sp. Parc Cae'r Felin. Cae Felin Parc.

Lit. meaning:- park of the mill field/enclosure.

CAE-GARW

Caegarw Cottage	1871	Cens.	Aberdare Library.
Caegarw	1881	ibid.	
Caegarw	c1890	MAP&A.39.	
Caegarw	1989	OS.	Pathfinder 1129.

Welsh 'cae' + 'garw'.

cae = a field.
garw = coarse, rough, rugged, harsh.

The name of the settlement in 1851 was *Allen's town* named after landowner I.H.Allen. His name is retained in the street name *Allen Street.*

pron. Kah-ee gah-roo [stress on the third syllable 'gah'].

Sp. Cae-garw.

Lit. meaning:- coarse field.

CARNETOWN

Parc Newydd	*1842-50*	*PRB Owner,Mrs.R.**Carne.***	
			HMH.112.
Parc Newydd	*1849*	*PRB Owner,Rev.R.**Carne.** SA.94.*	
Parc Newydd Colry.Co	*1864*	*MAP&A.17.*	
Carne Park Level	*1864*	*ibid.*	
Carnetown	*c.1900*	*MAP&A.54.*	
Carne Park Level	*c.1904*	*MAP&A.17.*	
Carnetown Mixed School	*1910.opnd. MAP&A.84-5.*		
Carnetown	*1919*	*OS*	*Ab'dare Libry.*
Carnetown	*1954*	*OS1".*	
Carnetown	*1964*	*HMH.103.*	
Carnetown	*1989*	*OS Landranger 170.*	

English 'Carne', pers. name + 'town'.

This part of *Abercynon* takes its name from the *Carne* family (see *Parc Newydd*, 1842-50 & 1849 above) an old Glamorgan landowning family.
The name *Carne* itself is Welsh in origin, reputedly from the place-name *Pencarn*, Monmouthshire, once the home of the family.
'carn' (cairn, burrow, tumulus, mound, rock, heap, pile etc. GPC). see Welsh Surnames.
The *Carne* family also had links with *Ewenni Priory*, *St.Donat's Castle* and *Nash* as well as *Carnetown*.
The earlier names for this land were *New Park* and *Parc-newydd*, both meaning the same. ['park' can be land enclosed for hunting, a pleasure ground or a field].
Parc-newydd was used officially as late as 1880, while the name *Carnetown* was in use by 1910, and in all probability, as early as 1900. (see above).
The planning and building of the properties at *Carnetown* took place during the last two decades of the 1900s. see TMC. sn.
For detailed accounts of other Glamorgan and Gwent place-names with this sort of formation see *The Masters of the Coalfield* by Michael Eyers.

Sp. Carnetown.

Literal meaning:- 'town (of the) Carne (family)'.

CEFN-Y-DON

Cefndon	1674	HPP.63	PNDH.7.20.
Kindon	1739	HPP.52	ibid.
Cefn Donn	1738-73	Welsh Peity.HMH.47.	
Cefndon	1765	PR	PNDH.7.20.
Kefndon	1773	ibid.	
Kendon(correctly Cefn y don).1805,1674			HB iv,65.ibid.
Cefndon	1840	TS.Penderyn.	
Kendon	1841	Census	ibid.
Cefn y don	1851	ibid.	
Kindon	1879	ERB	ibid.
Cendon	1905	HPP.15.	
Cefndon	1914	Kelly	ibid.
Cefn-y-don	1954	OS1".	
Cefn-y-don	1989	OS.Pathfinder 1108.	

Welsh 'cefn' + 'y' + 'ton' (mutated to 'don').

cefn = a ridge, back, butt.

y = the

ton = 'layland, green; sward - the grassy surface of land; green turf; pasture land; land left unploughed for many years'.

For *Kindon, Kendon,* ie. the loss of internal 'f',
cf. *Cyncoed,* Cardiff from original *Cefncoed,*
also *cender* for *cefnder* [male cousin],
cenffordd for *cefnffordd* [ridgeway, highway],
cenfor for *cefnfor* [ocean],
cenbant for *cefnbant* [saddle-backed] &
cenllwyth for *cefnllwyth* [back-burden, load].

Ton is a common element in Welsh place-names. Some other place-names in the Cynon valley containing this element are:
Tir y toncoch (red unploughed land); *Ton Dafydd Bengrych* (Dafydd Bengrych's [wavy hair] layland; *Ton glwyd-fawr* (big gate layland); *Ton llwyd,* (grey or poor layland); *Ty'n-y-ton* (layland small holding) and *Fforch-don* (layland fork).

pron. kevn ugh don.

Sp. Cefn-y-don.

Lit. meaning:- the layland ridge.

CEFNPENNAR

Keven Penare yssa	*1582*	*MR.PNC,Bangor.*	
Keven Penare ycha	*1582*	*ibid.*	
Keven Penarth	*1638*	*ibid.*	
Keven penarth	*1666*	*ibid.*	
Keven pennarth isha		*17th cent.Meisg.436.*	
Keven Pennarth		*17th.cent.ibid.*	
Cefn Pena	*1799*	*Yates.*	*CVAI.14.*
Cefnpennaruchaf	*1814*	*OS.*	*Aberdare Library.*
Cefnpennarisaf	*1814*	*ibid.*	
Cefn Pennar	*1844*	*TS.Aberdare.*	
Cefn Pennar Ychaf	*1844*	*ibid.*	
Cefn Pennar Isaf	*1844*	*ibid.*	
Cefnpennar	*1851*	*Census.*	*MR.PNC,Bangor.*
Cefnpennar	*1954*	*OS1".*	
Cefnpennar	*1989*	*OS.*	*Landranger 170.*

Welsh   'cefn' + 'pennar (dd) '.

cefn   = a mountain ridge.

pennar (dd) = highland.

[pen + ardd (height) or poss. pen + garth (ridge, wooded slope, hill).]

PS. When *garth* (ridge, wooded slope, hill) is a second or third element in a place-name it often mutates e.g. *Llwyn-arth, Llwyd-arth*, prob. *Penarth* etc. and is in most cases erroneously taken for 'arth' the bear. *Garth* and *Llwydarth* near Maesteg contain the same *garth* element with *llwyd* used to differentiate the one from the other.

pron. keven penn-ar.

Sp. Cefnpennar.

Lit. meaning:- highland ridge. [MR. PNC, Bangor.]

CWMPENNAR

Cwmpennar	*1799*	*Yates.*	*CVAI.14.*
Cwmpennar	*1850*	*Coal pits.*	*HMH.61.*
Cwmpennar	*1954*	*OS1".*	
Cwmpennar	*1989*	*OS*	*Landranger 170.*

Welsh   cwm + Pennar.

cwm   = valley.
Pennar = name of brook. cf. Aberpennar, Cwmpennar.
[The pennar stream takes its name from its source, the *Pennar* mountain].

pron. koom (as in "standard Eng." 'room') penn-ar.

Sp.Cwmpennar.

Lit. meaning:- Valley (of the) Pennar (brook).

CEFN RUGOS

Cefn Rhydgroes	1833	OS 1"	Reprint.
Cefn Rhigos	1954	OS 1".	
Cefn Rhigos	1991	OS	Landranger 160.

Welsh   cefn + rugos.

cefn   =   mountain ridge

rugos   =   place of heather. see Y Rugos.

rhydgroes of 1833 is most prob. the result of popular etymology. see *Y Rugos*.

The place-name element *cefn* is commmon throughout Wales because of the hilly nature of our country. It is also to be found in Cornwall as Cornish *keyn* in *Kenwyn* (white mountain ridge). In south east France it appears as '*les Cevennes*' (the mountain ridges), perhaps as a legacy of the Brythonic Celts of southern Germany in the east of Gaul (see Celts. 246). The Irish word for 'the human back' and 'mountain ridge' is *druim*. This element appears in its Welsh forms *trim* and *drum* in the place-names *Trimsaran* (Carms), *Meidrum* (Carms), *Coedrum* and *Drim woods* (Pembs), *Trum y Ddysgl* (Caerns), etc. It also appears tautologically with Welsh *cefn* in *Cefndrum* (Llandeilo Fach) *Cefn y drum* (Caerns) and *Kevendrym* (Pembs). *Cefn* was added to *drum* to explain the topography of a place whose name already meant mountain ridge.

The use of parts of the human body in Welsh place-names is widespread.eg.
Troed-y-rhiw (foot of the hill); *Y Bigwn*, (migwrn, [pigwrn, dial.] = ankle) a field name, Aberdare; *Bolgoed* (wood belly); *Brondeg* (fair breast); *Penderyn* (bird's head); *Llygad Cynon* (Cynon's eye, river source); *Trallwnc* (llwnc = throat, for a wet, damp place); *Trwyn Llwyd* (grey promontary, trwyn = nose) cf. poss. *Troon*, Scotland; *Braich yr hwch* (the sow's arm) Meir.; *Llawhaden* (llaw = hand) by popular etymology from original *Llanhuadain; Gwar y scwd*, Brecs. (above the waterfall, gwar = nape of the neck); *Y Fochriw,* Merthyr Tydfil (boch = cheek, ie. cheek shaped hill), etc. and of course *Cefn Rhigos.*

Pron. Keven Reegoss.

Sp. Cefn Rugos.

Lit. meaning:- heathery mountain ridge or, the mountain ridge of Rugos.

CWM CYNON

Cwmcynon forge	*17th.cent. HMH.41.*	
Cwmcynon	*1814*	*OS.* *Aberdare Library.*
Cwm Cynon	*1841*	*TS.Llanwynno.*
Cwmcynon	*1842-50*	*PRB.* *HMH.111.*
Cwmcynon coal pit	*1873*	*HMH.61.*
Cwmcynon Colliery	*1890*	*MAP&A.12.*
Cwmcynon Colliery	*1932*	*ibid.24.*
Cwm Cynon	*1989*	*OS Pathfinder 1129.*
Cwm Cynon Ind.Prk.	*1994*	

Welsh 'cwm' + 'Cynon'.

cwm = a valley.

Cynon = river name. (see *Abercynon*).

Cwm Cynon farm and forge became the site of *Cwmcynon Colliery* which in turn was demolished and the land transformed into the *Cwm Cynon Business Park.*

The place-name *Cwm Cynon* can be specific when referring to the above, but is also used generally for the district ie. *Cynon Valley.*

pron. koom kun-non.

Sp. Cwm Cynon.

Lit. meaning:- Valley (of the river) Cynon or Cynon Valley.

CWMAMAN

Cwm-Ammaan Farm (Y Llaethdy)	*1778*	*HCI 2.*
Cwm Amman House	*1778*	*ibid.*
Cwm Aman	*1836*	*HCI.1.*
Cwm Amman Colliery (Shepherd's Pit)	*1849*	*BN to 'GA'. 70.*
Cwmaman,Shepherds Arms,Fforchaman Rd	*1850*	*IHBHAD. 125.*
Cwmaman,Cwmneol Colliery (Morris Pit)	*1847-51*	*BN to'GA'. 70.*
Cwmaman	*1851*	*Cens.*
Cwmaman,Fforchaman Colliery (Brown's Pit)	*1852-58*	*BNto'GA'.70.*
Cwmaman,Vale of Neath Railway	*1857*	*HCI.9.*
Cwmaman,Zoar Chapel	*1859*	*OA. vol 1. 71.*
Cwmaman British School	*1862-67*	*HMH. 74.*
Cwmaman,a Reading Room For	*1868*	*AbdreTimes.HCI.*
Cwmaman,near Aberdare,South Wales	*1875*	*HCI.7.*
Cwmaman	*1878*	*WRG/SW..PNCB.*

Welsh. Cwm + Aman
Cwm = valley

Aman = name of river

Valley of the river Aman.

Cwm is a widely used element in Welsh place names, eg.*Cwm-bran, Cwmbach, Cwmtwrch* etc. and describes a bowl-shaped,cup-shaped or trough-shaped valley. This same element is to be found in English place-names as *combe*, eg. *Ilfracombe* (valley of the people of Ielfred), *Winscombe* (Wine's valley) etc.

The Welsh river-name *Aman(w)* is based on Welsh *banw*, a pig or pigling cf. Irish *banb*, and is used for a river rooting through the ground. (see *Aberaman*).

Blaenaman Fach and *Blaenaman Fawr (1799, Yates)* refer to the heads of the valleys of the lesser and larger *Aman* rivers respectively and later (via prob. *Tir Blaenaman Fawr/Fach)* the topographical names became the farm-names.

The confluence of the *Aman Fach* and *Aman Fawr* is at *Fforchaman.* (fork of the Aman). *Cwmneol, Fforchneol, Y Llaethdy* [esgair y llaith tir, 'the ridge of the damp land' in 1570 has become llaethdy, 'the dairy', lit. milk house, by the 17th cent. Llaith (damp, moist) was prob. confused with the more common llaeth (milk)] and *Pwllfa* were the other farms of pre-industrial *Cwmaman*.

Moel yr Hyddod (bare, rounded hill of the stags) was the earlier(1570) name for the land of *Blaenaman Fawr*. Local dial. pron. 'mol'. cf. *y Vole*, Penderyn and *Malvern* (Moel-fryn), Worcs.

The opening of the three coalmines (listed above), the first in 1849, started the development of an industrial settlement at the head of the *Aman* Valley (lit. *Blaenaman*).
Cwmaman Colliery was also known as *Shepherd's Pit* (named after the owner) and the *Shepherds Arms* (opened 1850) also bears his name. *Morris St.* apparently is named after the owner of *Cwmneol Colliery* which was also called *Morris Pit*. *Fforchaman Colliery* was called *Brown's Pit*, again named after its owner.

Cwmaman, as in *Cwmaman Farm, House and Colliery,* became the name of the village.

pron. koom <u>am</u> an. cwm<u>am</u>an.

Sp. Cwmaman.

Literal meaning:- Valley of the river Aman.

CWM-BACH

Cwmbach	*1788. 1823*	*BFR.OA.vol vii.11.*
Cwmbach	*1802*	*PR.Aberdare Library.*
Cwmbach	*1833*	*OS.36. MR.PNC,Bangor.*
Pit sank at Cwmbach	*1837*	*HMH.57.*
Cwmbach	*1841*	*Cens. Ab'dare Libry.*
Cwm-bach	*1844*	*TS.Aberdare.*
Cwmbach	*1847 Commission on Ed.in Wales.*	
	*HMH.75."From this **hamlet**.."*	
Cwm Bach	*1853 Rammell. O.A. vol.1. p46.(300 or 400*	
		houses).

Cwmbach Society.(Coop.) 1860   Abdre.Coop.Soc. OA.vol.7.29.
Miss Sarah Williams,Cwmbach.1855-65 Telynog 113.
Cwmbach   *1919   OSM 25".*
Cwmbach Pit(disused)   1919   OSM 25".
Cwmbach Little Pit(disused) 1919   OSM 25".
Cwmbach Junction.[TVR]   1919   OSM 25".

Welsh   Cwm + bach.

Small or little valley.

'Cwm' is a valley shaped as a trough, dish or bowl.

'Bach' is an adjective meaning 'little' or 'small'.

Cwm-bach was the name given to a farmstead in 'the little valley' and the earliest recorded names refer to the farmstead.
In 1844, the area we know today as *Cwm-bach* consisted of the following farms or homesteads:-
Ynyscynon (Cynon river meadow). see *Ynyscynon*. *Pant y Gerddinen* (hollow of the rowan tree). The name survives today in *Pant Farm, Gerdinen Terrace and Pant y Cerdin*. *Werfa* (shaded place); *Blaen-nant-y-groes* (head, source of the *Nant-y-groes*); *Abernant-y-groes Ychal/Isha* (confluence of the Nant-y-groes, higher/lower farms); *Ty llwyd* (grey or holy house); *Tir y Founder* (land of the metal caster); *Tir bach* (small farmstead); *Llety Shencyn* (Shencin's lodge/abode) and *Cwm-bach*.
With the development of the *Aberdare Canal* (1812-1900), the sinking of coal pits in the area (1837-50) and the coming of rail transport, an industial settlement grew rapidly from the middle of the 19th century and adopted the name of the original *Cwm-bach* farm.
In 1860 the first Cooperative in Wales was formed at Bridge Road, *Cwmbach*
Telynog (Thomas Evans) the poet lived in *Cwmbach* and worked in *Llety Shencyn Pit* until his untimely death in 1865, aged 25 years. He wrote the ode to Miss Sarah Williams, Cwmbach (1855-65). *Tre Telynog* is named after him.
Cwm-bach is a common place-name,e.g.
Cwm-bach, Glasbury, Powys; *Cwm-bach*, Llanelli, Dyfed; *Cwm-bach*, Llanwinio, Dyfed; *Cwm Bach,* Breudeth (Brawdy), Dyfed etc.

pron. koom-baach(guttral 'ch'). cwm-b<u>ach</u>.

Sp. Cwm-bach.
Literal meaning :-   little valley.

CWMDÂR   CWMDARE

Tir Kwmdaer	*1638*	*CFL. Glam. MR. PNC,Bangor.*
Tir Cwmdaer	*1666*	*CR ii. 90. ibid.*
Cwmdare	*1680*	*JAI iv. ibid.*
Cwmm daer		*17th.Cent.RJT. Meisg.436.*
Cwmdare	*1748*	*PR. Aberdare Library.*
Cwmdare Vechan	*1766*	*BFR. SAPN.11.*
Cwmdare now Tyr y Bwllva	*1778*	*ibid.*
Cwmdare Hamlet	*1778*	*ibid.*
Cwm Dare	*1833*	*OS 36. MR. PNC,Bangor.*
Cwmdare	*1954*	*OS1".*
Cwmdare	*1989*	*OS. Landranger 170.*
Dare Valley Country Park	*1989*	*ibid.*

Welsh. 'cwm' + 'Dâr / Dare'.

cwm = 'a deep narrow valley, coomb, glen, dale;
    hollow, bowl shaped depression;' GPC.
    cf. Irish 'cum' (vessel), Breton, 'komm' (trough, shallow
    vessel), Gaulish, 'cumba' (the bottom of a ship).
    see PNDPH. sn. 339. also see Cwmaman.

Dâr, Dare = river name. see *Aberdare, Bwllfa Dare.*

Over the last 200 years, *Cwmdare* has changed from a pastoral hamlet, to a mining village and ultimately to a residential area and a country park.

pron. koom dahr, (as in Eng. 'car' with rolled 'r'): see *Aberdâr/Aberdare.*

Sp. Cwmdâr, Cwmdare.

Lit. meaning:-   Valley (of the river) Dare.

CWM YNYSMINTAN

Ynys Mintan	1787	83 PR.	*PNDH.7.35.1.*
Ynis y myntan	1799	ibid.	
Cwm ynis y mintan	1802	ibid.	
Cwmynysminton	1809-36	OSM 1809-36. Meisg.72.	
Cwm.? winton	1841	cens.	*PNDH.7.35.1.*
Cwmynysmintan	1861 & 71.cens.	ibid.	
Cwmsmintan	1905	HPP.15.	
Cwmynysmintan	1905	HPP.79.	
Cwm Smintan	1922	LYH.117.	
Cwm Ynys mintan	1954	OSI".	
Cwmynysmintan	1995	MSP.Aberdare.	

Welsh   'cwm' + 'ynys' + 'mintan'.
cwm   = valley.
ynys   = river meadow.
mintan = obscure element

The third element *mintan* is slightly problematic, but the indications are that it could be the surname *Minton* (see 1809-36 forms).
The local dialect would account for the *ton* becoming *tan,*
cf. *gelynen* > *gelynan* (Fforch Neuol, TS. 236. Ty Llwyd, TS. 938.);
Hatton > *Hatan* (Tir y Founder.); *darren* > *darran* (Ynys-lwyd.);
tyle > *tila* (Tila Robert.); *Hepste* > *Hepsta* (LYH. 118.);
pompren > *pompran* (LYH. 119.); *Ystradfellte* > *Ystradfellta* (HPP.93.)
cefen > *cefan* (Tir Draw,1094.); *Y Dylles* > *Y Dyllas,* etc.

The use of the definite article 'y' (the) before the element [as in 1799 & 1802] is, at times, used with pers. names. cf. *Tir y Ioryn* (Iorwerth); *y Guto* (Gruffydd); *y Bedo* (Meredydd), etc. (see Meisg.75).

Names & surnames used in the 1844 TS are :-
Ynis Crysby, Aberaman Isaf; *Cae Soudon,* Waun Soudon; *Erw Harry; Cae Coulson; Cae Smith; Cae Dd.N.John; Cae Lewis; Caia Mary Morgan,* Ty Draw; *Cae Watkin Jones,* Gwrid; *Cae Jacky,* Hirwaun Common; *Tir Evan Bach Traws; Cae Wm. Morgan,* Ffynnon y Gog; *Tila Robert; Cae Gutto,* Ysgubor Wen; *Tre Gibbon; Cae Evan;Caia Dd.Watkins,* Llwydcoed Est.; *Cae Dd.y Cridd,* Tir Mawr; *Cae Cristinas,* Abernant-y-groes Ychaf (cf. Blaen-nant-y-groes, 23.); *Island Dafydd,* Ynys Llwyd; *Cae Evan Morgan,* Cefn Cynon; *Caia Wayne; Cae Griffith;*

Cae Llewellyn; Cae Morgan; Cae Wayne; Cae Morris; Cae Samuel Thomas; Cae Cullimore, all Gadlys Est. *Cae Llewellyn Isaf,* Abercwmboy Farm; *Ton Dafydd Pen Gegel,* Ton Coch; *Tir y Founder; Lletty Shenkin; Gwain Shenkin,* Abergwawr; *Waun Gwillim,* Bwllfa; *Moss Row Field,* Blaennant; *Tir y Bailey; Tir Gwyn Bach (poss.); Tir Nant y Maden; Cae Howell; Wern Batty,* Cefndon; *Cwm Nant Iorath,* Ffrwd Isha; *Pwll Howell; Gwern Ivor; Tir Howell Laythog; Ynis Meurig & Penrhiw Gradoc.*

Minton is a Shropshire surname and is a combination of Welsh *mynydd > mynd* and Old Eng. *tun,* (myndton > minton) meaning 'mountain farm'. see PDS. sn.

[Ironmaster John Thompson from Shropshire was one of the founders of the Aberdare Ironworks at *Llwydcoed.* c1800. Could *Minton* have been a pioneer?]

The name *Minton* does not appear in births, deaths or marriages recorded in the Aberdare Parish Register for 1735-1808.

The 1905 and 1922 forms of *smintan* are an example of an abbreviated *ynys,* as a residual 's'. cf. *Sketty* from *Ynys Ceti.*

However, it is possible that the third element is Welsh *mintan* = argue ['as in Glamorgan speech'. GPC.]. cf. *Llwyn y dadlau., see Gadlys.*

It is also possible that it is Welsh *mintan* = mint, ie. *ynys mintan* meaning the river meadow where mint grows. [see Gelli Dafolog].

pron. koom ughniss mintan. cwm y̲n̲ys mintan.

BFR informs me that the local pron. is still cwm smintan.

Sp. Cwm Ynysmintan.

Lit. meaning:- poss. valley (of) Minton's river meadow,
       or valley of the mint meadow,
       or valley of the meadow of argument.

Y DARRAN-LAS

Tarenlas	*1814*	*OS.*	*Aberdare Library.*
Darran Las	*1841*	*TS.*	*Llanwynno.*
Darranlas	*1842-50*	*PRB.*	*HMH.111.*
Darrenlas	*1851*	*Cens.*	*Aberdare Library.*
Darranlas	*1989*	*OS.*	*Pathfinder 1129.*

Welsh   'tarren' (mutated to 'darren' after lost def. art. 'y'.)
    +   'glas' (mutated to 'las', adj. following fem. noun.).

tarren = 'hill, land which has rock near the surface'. BFR.
           'tump, knoll, ridge'. BGC.
           'a thin layer of soil on a rock that bakes and becomes barren
           in the sun'. Ell. 'rock, knoll, tump'. GM.
        darran is the local dial.pron.of *darren.*

glas   = 'green; blue; pale; grey; young, raw;'. GM.
         usually 'green' when referring to vegetation & land.
         eg. *bryn glas* (green hill); *coed glas* (green wood); *cau glas*
         (green hollow,as in *Glasgow*); *cae glas* (green field); *porfa las*
         (green pasture), etc.

However, a visit to *Darran-las* in late spring and early summer will probably reveal the true etymology of the name as the mountainside has a blue hue provided by a mass of bluebells.

pron. ugh dah-ran(rolled 'r') lah-ss (rhymes with Eng. 'farce'[silent 'r']).

Sp. Y Darran-las.

Lit. meaning:- the blue rocky outcrop.

DYFFRYN

Dyffryn House　　　　*1699*　　*SAPN.12.*
Dyffryn,furnace　　　*17th cent. HMH.41.*
Dyffryn House　　　　*1738-73　Welsh Piety.　HMH.47.*
Duffrin Aberdaer　　　*1799*　　*Yates.*　　*CVAI.14.*
Dyffryn　　　　　　　*1814*　　*OS.*　　*Ab'dare Lib'ry.*
Dyffryn Arms　　　　*1830*　　*IHBHAD.sn.*
Dyffryn　　　　　　　*1844*　　*TS.Aberdare.*
Dyffryn Arms　　　　*1844*　　*ibid.*
Duffryn,Old,Lower,Middle,Upper.Thos.Powel Collieries.1850-63.
　　　　　　　　　　　　　　　　　　　　　　　　APP.41c.

Duffryn,Deep　　　*c1850s.*　*APP.41a.*
Powell Duffryn Co.　*1866*　　*APP.vol.1.49.*
Duffryn,Compagnie Francaise de Mines Powell.1914. APP.vol.1.66.
Dyffryn　　　　　　　*1954*　　*OS1".*
Parc Duffryn Pennar　1995　　*Aberdare Leader.*

Welsh　　dyffryn < 'dwfr' (water) + 'hynt' (way, course).
dyffryn = valley, vale bottom.
The name *Dyffryn* in the Cynon Valley has pastoral, industrial, political, social as well as educational links. Pastoral re. the early farm, mill and *Dyffryn woods*; industrial re. the coal mines and the vast *Powell Duffryn company;* political and educational re. *Dyffryn House,* the home of Henry Austin Bruce (1815-95), first *Baron Aberdare of Dyffryn,* Home Secretary 1869-73; Chancellor, University of Wales, 1892-95; also educational re. *Dyffryn House,* later to house the *Montain Ash Grammar/Comprehensive Schools,* and social re. the *Dyffryn Arms* and *Parc Dyffryn Pennar.*

'dwfr' is to be found in place-names such as *Dover, Andover,*
　　　　Candover, Wendover, etc.
Hynt meaning a way or course is to be found in other place-names
eg. *Epynt* = 'eb' (horse, as in 'ebol') + 'hynt' meaning a place where horses would run a course.
Gabrosentum, in Romano-British Cumberland is a combination of the British forms of the Welsh words *gafr* (goat) and *hynt,* indicating a passage for goats.
Y Gerrynt, Gwynedd. The second element is *hynt.* The first is obscure.
see ELlSG.110

There is a tendency to associate *dyffryn* with the valley bottom, the low part of a river valley.

The site of *Deep Duffryn Colliery* has been reclaimed, landscaped and is now known as *Parc Dyffryn Pennar,* the home ground of *Mountain Ash RFC.*

pron. duff-rin (rolled 'r').

Sp. Dyffryn.

Lit. meaning:- a river valley.

Y DYLLAS

Dullest	*1814*	*OS.*	*Aberdare Library.*
Waun Dyllas	*1844*	*TS.*	*Aberdare.*
Dyllas Cottages	*1861*	*Cens.*	*Aberdare Library.*
Dullas Colliery	*1896*	*OA.vol.1.21.*	
Dyllas Colliery	*1914*	*APP.vol.2.*	
Dyllas Farm	*1989*	*OS. Pathfinder 1109.*	
Dyllas Cottage	*1989*	*ibid.*	

Welsh   'y' + 'tyllest'.

y   = the

tyllest = form, formation, shape.

It is very difficult to form a firm opinion without the early forms of this place-name, but if the 1814 name is accurate, then one can deduce :-
  1. a meaning of a 'formation', prob. geological.
  2. a lair, a den, a hole. (BFR.)
  3. a stone quarry. (RJT)
  4. a shady place. (RJT).
cf. Tarran y Dyllas (Llantrisant), Meisg. 202.
Y Dyllas is local dial. pronounciation with -es -> -as. (cf. *Ynys Mintan*).

In Welsh (locally) the name is always **Y** *Dyllas,* cf. other place-names that retain the article e.g. *Y Gadlys, Y Bala, Y Fenni, Y Bont,* etc. The article is also retained by English-speakers as *the Dyllas, the Gadlys* etc.

pron. ugh dill ('ll' as in Llanelli) ass.

Sp. Y Dyllas.

Lit. meaning obscure.

FOUNDRY TOWN

Foundry Town   *1861*   *Cens.*   *Aberdare Library.*
Foundry Town   *1885*   *OSM25".*
Foundry Town   *1900*   *OSM25".*
Foundry Town   *1992*   *CVOH.*

English   'foundry' + 'town'.

foundry   'the art of founding or casting;
                a place where founding is carried on'. CED.
town   'a populous place'. CED.

'*The Dare foundry* was in *Elizabeth St.* backing on to *Seion Chapel* now
the car park opposite the police station. The area usually regarded as
Foundry Town includes the area south of *Wind St.* - west of *Nant Row* -
through *Monk St.* to include *Clifton St.* and *Pendarren St.*' (TE).

Sp. Foundry Town.

Lit. meaning:- town (of the) foundry.

FFORCHAMAN

forche Aman	*1570*	*SAPN.12.*	
fforghe Aman	*1594*	*ibid.*	
tire fforch Amman	*1666*	*ibid.*	
tir fforch amann	*17th cent.*	*Meisg.436.*	
Fforchamman Hamlet	*1778*	*SAPN.12.*	
Fforchamman	*1814*	*OS.*	*Aberdare Library.*
Forchaman	*1841*	*Census.*	*ibid.*
Fforch Amman	*1844*	*TS.Aberdare.*	
Fforchaman Colliery	*1856*	*HCI.8-9.*	
Fforchaman Colliery	*1965*	*ibid.10.*	
Fforchaman Rd.& St.	*1995*	*MSP.Aberdare.*	

Welsh. 'fforch' + 'Aman'.

fforch = fork, from Latin 'furca'.
      (Eng. 'fork, pitchfork, prong'). GPC.
As a place-name element:-
'the meeting place of two streams in the form of a two pronged fork, with the on-going river/stream forming the shaft'. Meisg. 26. (trans.)

Aman = river name. see Aberaman.

cf. *Fforchneuol* (below) and *Fforchwen* (white-fork) *Colliery*, 1897.

pron. fforch (rolled 'r' and guttral 'ch') am-an.

Sp. Fforchaman.

Lit. meaning:- (the) fork or meeting place (of the two) Aman (streams).

FFORCHNEUOL, FFORCH-WEN and CWMNEUOL

Tir Dafydd Sais	*1570*	*HCl.2.*
tir ddauydd Sais	*17th.cent.*	*Meisg.*
Tyr Fforchneole	*1771*	*SAPN.12.*
Tyr Forch Neyoll	*1778*	*ibid.*
Tir Fforch Nyoll	*1788*	*ibid.*
Cwmniol	*1814*	*OS. Aberdare Library.*
Tirdafiddsais	*1814*	*ibid.*
Fforchneuol	*1833*	*Colby. Meisg.72.*
Fforch Neuol	*1844*	*TS.Aberdare.*
Cwm Neuol	*1844*	*ibid.*
Y Fforchniol	*1854*	*GA. Meisg.72.*
Fforchniol	*1855*	*SAPN.12.*
Cwmneol coal pit	*1847*	*HCl.5.*
Cwmneol Inn	*1866*	*IHBHAD.sn.*
Fforchneol Colliery	*1868*	*HCl.10.*
Fforchneol Arms	*1872*	*IHBHAD.*
Fforchwen Colliery	*1897*	*APP.*
Craig Fforchneol	*1989*	*OS. Pathfinder 1109.*
Cwmneol Farm	*1989*	*ibid.*

Welsh   'fforch' (see *Fforchaman*) + 'Neuol'.
        'cwm' (see *Cwmbach*) + 'Neuol'
Neuol = river name. etymology obscure.

poss. both *Fforchneuol* and *Cwmneuol* were once part of *Tyr Dafydd Sais**. (Dafydd the English speaker or Englishman's land.)
*In a Welsh speaking community an English speaker is called a 'saes'. He need not neccessarily be an Englishman ie. a person born in England. He may consider himself an Englishman, or on the other hand, he may consider himself as an English speaking Welshman.

FFORCHNEUOL.

pron. fforch (as in Fforchaman) nay-ol. fforch <u>neu</u>ol.
local pron. fforch <u>nee</u>-ol.

Sp. unsure. Fforchneuol or Fforchneol. (Early spellings suggest neuol).

Lit. meaning:- (the) fork (of the) Neuol/Neol (brook).

CWMNEUOL.

pron. koom nay-ol.

Sp. Cwmneuol.

Lit. meaning:- (the) valley (of the) Neuol (brook).

FFORCH-WEN.

pron. fforch wen.

Sp. Fforch-wen.

Lit. meaning:- (the) white fork. cf. Hafod-wen.

Y GADLYS

Tir y gadlys ycha,yssa	*1632*	*SAPN.13.*
Y Gadlys	*1631*	*ibid.*
Gadles	*1666*	*HMH.42.*
Tir y gadlys ycha a		
thir y gadlys isha	*17th,Cent.*	*Meisg.434.*
Gadlas Ycha formerly Tyr y dadley	*1778*	*ibid.*
Gadlas isha,ycha	*1788*	*ibid.*
Gadlys Ironworks	*1827*	*CVAI.26.*
Gadlys,New Pit	*1844*	*APP.vol.1.60.*
Gadlys Estate	*1844*	*TS.Aberdare.*
Gadlys Ychaf	*1844*	*ibid.*
Gadlys Arms,Robertstown	*1852*	*IHBHAD.*
Gadlys Uchaf Tin Works	*1868*	*CVAI.32.*
Gadlys New Pit	*1875*	*OS.Aberdare.*
Gadlys Ward.(local govt.)	*1894*	*OA.vol.7.102.*
Gadlys,Bethel	*1897*	*OA.vol.1.13.*
Gadlys	*1954*	*OS1".*
Gadlys	*1989*	*OS Landranger 170.*

Welsh   'y' + 'cad' + 'llys'.
'y' = the.
'cad' = 1. battle, army. 2. hare.
'llys' = stockade, hedge, court.

cadlys, originally referred to a defensive place or a place strengthened and made secure by ditches and hedges. (see ELlSG.121). The Welsh equivalent of a 'motte and bailey' (as in castle) would have been 'tomen a *chadlys*'. Gradually *cadlys* (like the Eng. 'bailey') became a term for enclosed land, enclosure, courtyard or farm.
cf. the use of *bailey*. (see SAPN.13.) also cf. *cadlan*.

Llwyn y dadley (the dispute, discussion bush) is interesting. BFR informs me that 'dadlau' infers a legal dispute - more like a court. It could poss. be land that was the subject of dispute. cf. Y Dadleu Dy (Llantrisant) trans. as 'the Court House', see Meisg. 105.

Other examples of *gadlys* are:-
Gadlys, Mynytho; *Y Gadlys*, Llanwnda; *Tan y Gadlas*, Bethesda; *Ty'n y Gadlas*, Carmel, Cilgwyn & *Y Gadlys*, Llangynnwyd.

pron. gad-liss.

Sp. Y Gadlys.

Lit. meaning:- the enclosed land, courtyard, farm.

GELLI-DAFOLOG

Gelli Dyfolas	1777	PR.	PNDH.7.52.
Gelli dy volas	1783	ibid.	
Gellidavollus	1836	ERB.	PNDH.7.52.
Gelli Davolas	1830	OS.	
Gelli Davolas	1840	TM.	
Gellydafolog	1861 & 71.cens.	PNDH.7.52.	
Gellidyfolws	1905	HPP.13.	
Gelli Diafolws	1905	ibid.	
GellydafolaS	1926	Kelly.	PNDH.7.52.
Gelli-dafolog	1905	OS6".	ibid.
Gelli-dafolog	1989	OS.	Pathfinder 1108.

Welsh   'celli' + 'tafolog'.

celli = 'grove, copse of trees, bushes; woodland, wooded glade'.

tafolog =   'of dock plants'. 'tafol' + adjectival suffix '-og'.
tafolas,
tafolws = 'dock plants'. 'tafol' + old collective suffix '-os'.
        '-os' > '-as' eg. *bedwos > Bedwas;*
                        Onnos   > Annas;
                Y Wernos Deg > Y Wernas Deg;
                        Derwos > Derwas.   Ell. 51.
        '-os' > '-ws' eg. *Trebanos > Trebanws;*
            cf. *Trebannog*, Penderyn and *Trebanws*, Cwm Tawe.

celli, y gelli, is a common Welsh place-name element.
Examples in the Cynon Valley are:-
Y Gelli Bêr, (pêr = sweet, delicious, lucious);
Y Gelli Dawal, (tawel = quiet, peaceful);
Y Gelli Fendigaid, (bendigaid = blessed);
Y Gelli Deg, (teg = fair, beautiful);
Gelli ben-uchel, (pen uchel = top end);
Gelli-fach, (bach = small, dear, endearing);
Gelli Ffynhonnau, (ffynhonnau = springs, wells);
Gelli Neuadd, (neuadd = hall, residence);
Gelli Tarw, (tarw = bull);
Gelli Ddu, (du = black);
Gelli Fanaches, (mynaches = nun);
Gelli Wrgan, (Gwrgan = pers. name) and
Gelli-lwch, (llwch = lake).

tafolog a composite word containing *tafol* (dock plant) + adjectival suffix
'-og', means a place of dock plants.
cf. *Tafolog* and *Afon Dafolog*, Gwynedd. (ELlSG.33.)
Similar plant place-names are:-
eithinog (furze,gorse);
haiddog (barley, cf. Haydock Park);
grugog (heather) cf. *Y rugos, Rhigos*;
banhadlog, banalog (broom);
brwynog (rushes); *celynnog* (holly); *rhedynog* (ferns);
ysgallog (thistles),etc.

tafolos, -ws, is the old collective form of the noun tafol, *-tafolos.*
Tafolws is prob.local pron. The present day plural form is *tafol* with
tafolen as the fem. sing. cf. *pebyll* old sing. form with *pebyllau* as
plural. Today *pabell* is the sing. form and *pebyll* the plural. also cf.
plantos (little children[Anwyl]), gwrageddos (gossips, silly women
[Anwyl]).
Similar place-names with the old collective suffix '-os' are:-
Gwernos (alders) eg. *Y Wernos Deg,* Beddgelert;
Trebanos (pan = cotton grass);
Bedwos (birches) eg. *Bedwas,* Caerffili;
Grugos (heathers), *Y Rugos;*
Helygos (willows) eg. *Lygos*,Clydach,Cwm Tawe;
Gwastad Onnos (ash trees), etc.
Field names in the Cynon valley with plant elements in the 1844 TS
were:-
melarian (valerian, all-heal), Aberaman Ychaf; *Bryn syfi, Cae syfi*
(strawberry) Pantygerddinen, Aberffrwd, Dyffryn; *Cae'r rye grass,*
Pantygerddinen; *cae fetchys* (vetch field), Blaennant; *cae gwinydd*
(woodbine, honeysuckle), Cwm du, Ynys Llwyd; *cae ysgallog* (thistle),
Ysgubor Wen & others; *cae rhyg* (rye), Ysguborwen; *caia eirhinog*
[eirinog] (bearing plums, damsons; sloes, bullace or berries) Tir y Iorin;
caia eithin (furze, gorse) Tir y Iorin & others; *cae haidd* (barley),
Dyffryn Dâr & others; *cae'r pys* (peas), Llwyn Helyg; *potato garden,*
Llwydcoed Est. & others; *cae'r gwenith* (wheat), Fforch Aman & others;
ceirch (oats), Pwllfa & others; *Waun clovers,* Ynys Llwyd; *Glyn y*
rhedyn (fern),Vedw Hir; *ynys y trwne* [trewynau] (loosestrife),
Abercwmboi; *banwen* [panwaun] cotton-grass,general; *cae cawn* (reeds),
Dyffryn; *cae'r fallan* (apple), Wern Fawr & *coedcae ffa'r palog* (stick
beans), Ffrwd Genol Fach.

pron. gelli ('g' as in Eng.'got'; elli rhymes with Llanelli) dah-vole ogg.

Sp. Gelli-dafolog.

Lit. meaning:- wooded glade of dock plants.

GLANCYNON

Glancynon Foundry,Aberdare	*1828*	*APP.vol.2.17.*
Glan-cynon Foundry	*1885*	*OS25".*
Glancynon Inn,Hirwaun	*c1875*	*PNDH.*
Glancynon Inn,Trecynon	*1867*	*IHBHAD.*
Glancynon,Abercynon	*c1930*	*MAP&A.61.*

Welsh 'glan' + 'Cynon'.
glan = 'edge, brink; shore, bank; rising ground, hillside'.
Cynon = river name. see *Abercynon.*

The sense of on the 'bank of the Cynon' would be appropriate to these four identical place-names from different locations in the valley. In *Hirwaun, Trecynon, Aberdare* and *Abercynon,* they all are or were on the bank of the *Cynon* river.
cf. *Glandare* (bank of the Dare). *Glanynys* (edge of the river meadow). *Ynys Glandwr* (river meadow on the water's edge). *Glanffrwd* (bank of the ffrwd [brook]).
In many Welsh place-names, *glan* has been confused with and erroneously replaced by *llan.*
eg. *Llanbradach* was originally *Glanbradach* (bank of the Bradach brook).
   Llancaeach was originally *Glancaeach* (bank of the Caeach brook).
   Llanmarlais was *Glanmarlais*; *Llandafen* was *Glandafen,* etc.
This was due to the mutated *glan* becoming *lan* and being mistakenly interpreted as *llan.*
There are no examples of this change in the *glan* names of the Cynon Valley.

pron. glan <u>cun</u> on.

Sp. Glancynon.

Lit. meaning:- (on the) bank (of the river) Cynon.

GODREAMAN

Godreaman	*1871*	*Census.*	*Aberdare Library.*
Godreaman	*1989*	*OS. Pathfinder 1109.*	
Godreaman St.	*1995*	*MSP.Aberdare.*	

Welsh.   'godre' + 'Aman'.
godre = 'boundary, bottom, foot of mountain or hill'.
Aman. = river name. see Aberaman.
cf. *Godre'r Graig*, Cwm Tawe.

pron. god re ('e' as in 'men') am an. (emphasis on 'am'). godre am̲a̲n.

Sp. Godreaman.

Lit. meaning:- bottom end (of the) Aman (river/valley).

GWERNIFOR

Gwern Ifor	*1814*	*OS.*	*Aberdare Library.*
Gwern Ifor	*1833*	*OS1".*	*reprint.*
Gwernifor	*1842-50*	*PRB.*	*HMH.111.*
Gwern Ivor	*1841*	*TS.*	*Llanwynno.*
Gwaun Ivor	*1851*	*Cens.*	*Aberdare Library.*
Gwernifor St.	*1995*	*MSP.*	

In the absence of early forms one can only assume the accuracy of the above.
Welsh   'gwern' + 'Ifor'.
gwern = 'boggy land; wet marshy land where alder trees grow'. RJT.
gwernen =   alder tree, gwern = alder trees and as they grow in wet marshy land, 'gwern' has also acquired the meaning of wet, marshy land'.
see PNDPH. sn.
'alder grove, alder marsh, swamp, quagmire; damp meadow'. GPC.

pron. gwern ('gw' & 'e' as in 'men' & rolled 'r')
     ee-vor (emphasis on 'ee').   gwern̲i̲for.

Sp. Gwernifor.

Lit. meaning:- Ifor's alder marsh.

HAFOD

Tir y Vodwen		*17th.cent. Meisg.436.*
Tir y Fodwen	*1788*	*SAPN.*
Hafodwen	*1854*	*ibid.*
Hafod Genol	*1841*	*TS. Llanwynno.*
Hafod Ucha	*1841*	*ibid.*
Hafod Fawr	*1841*	*ibid.*
Glyn hafod	*1993*	*SAPN.*
Glynhafod St.	*1995*	*MSP.Cwmaman.[Aberdare]*

Welsh   'haf', summer + 'bod', residence, abode.
hafod = 'summer dwelling; upland farm, occupied in the
    summer only; dairy house'. cf. 'hafdre' and 'hafoty'.
Hendre, hendy were the Welsh names for the main or winter farmhouses.
Hafod, hafdre (as in *Ynys hafdre* > *Ynysawdre*,Tondu. GP.WM.) and
hafoty were related to the farm houses that were used in summer only,
when the cattle and sheep were able to graze on the highland pasture.

The *vodwen* in *Tir y Vodwen* (land of the white summer dwelling) is
almost certainly *Hafod-wen*, and is so named in OS1" 1854. *Tir Hafod-
wen* suggests a more established settlement.   Probably the summer
dwelling became a small-holding in its own right.

Glynhafod means the valley of the summer farm and prob. refers to the
valley that connects *Blaenaman Fach* with *Hafod-wen*.   Is it a
coincidence that in 1844, the landowner of Blaenaman fach was a certain
Lady Glyn?
Hafod Genol (dial. for 'ganol') Eng. 'middle', *Hafod Ucha,* Eng.'upper'
and *Hafod Fawr*, Eng. 'big, great', are all in Llanwynno Parish.

pron.   ha vode ('o' as in Eng. 'door').

Sp. Hafod.

Lit. meaning:- summer residence.

HIRWAUN

Hyrweuunworgan	*1203*	*BMW iii. MR.PNC,Bangor.*
Hyrwenunworgan	*1203*	*Margam,174. Meisg.75.*
Hyrwen-worgan	*1253*	*Margam,267. Meisg.75.*
Hyrwenwurgan	*1256*	*Cart.Glam.II. 614.Meisg.75.*
Hirwen Urgan	*1536-9*	*Leland. MR.PNC,Bangor.*
Hirwein Vrgan	*1578*	*Glam.Ants. 113.Meisg.75.*
Hyre wenn Worgan	*1622-23*	*Plymouth. MR.PNC,Bangor.*
Hirwen Wrgan	*1638*	*CFL.Glam. MR.PNC,Bangor.*
Hirwainwrgan	*1729*	*Bowen. OA.vol i.cover.*
Tyr wain Wrgan,otherwise Hirwain Wrgan.1757 CVAI 13.		
Hirwainwrgan	*1760*	*EB/MSW. MR.PNC,Bangor.*
Hirwen	*1772-73*	*Welch Piety. Meisg.75.*
Hirwain Furnace	*1799*	*Yates's map.CVAI 14.(opened 1757).*
Hirwayn Wrgan Common. 1799		*Yates's map. CVAI 14.*
Cefn Hirwain	*1799*	*Yates's map. CVAI 14.*
Hirwaun Wrgan	*1833*	*Colby. Meisg.75.*
Hirwaun Common and Town.1844 TS,Aberdare.		
Irvan	*1862*	*George Borrow,Wild Wales, 502.*
Hirwaun	*1954*	*OSI".*

Welsh   'hir' (long) + 'gwaun' (plain, moorland field, meadow, moor,
down).

+ Wrgan, Gwrgant (pers. name).

Meaning:-   Gwrgant's long moor.

One cannot specify with certainty the identity of this particular *Gwrgant*.
Local historians have linked the name to that of *Wrgant ab Ithel* whose
son *Iestyn* was the last king of *Glamorgan*. This popular hypothesis has
been responsible for the names of *Iestyn Street* and *Broniestyn Terrace*.
However *Gwrgant* was a very popular name in Medieval Wales, eg.
*Gwrgant Mawr, G. ap Cynfyn ap Peibo, G. ap Gwynan, G. ap Ffyrnfael
ab Ithael, G. ap Meirchiawn, G. ap Dwnna, Gwrgant ab Ithael [Gurcant
filius ithail immolauit/uillam tref ginhill* (gwyngil?)*], Gwrgant, Bishop of
Llandaf (c.1148), G. Brydydd ap Rhys, pencerdd Morgan ab Owain o
Wynllwg etc.* (GBGG. sn.) and one needs more evidence to substantiate
the local hypothesis.
Indeed, it is also possible that the *Gwrgant* named was *Gwrgant* the

Bishop of Llandaf (c.1148) as the church does have a history as landowner in the parish.

cf. *Aberdare.* "For nearly 400 years the *Diocese of Gloucester* received the rent for the ground called *Maesydre** and when the ground was built on in the 1850's this fact was commemorated in the names of the streets such as *Gloucester St.Canon St. and Dean St.; Hall, Whitcombe, Weatherall* and *Seymour* were persons connected with the Diocese and *Pembroke St.* was named after *Pembroke College* Oxford, whose master was a Canon of *Gloucester.*" APP. vol. 1. p6.

**Maesydre* = *the town field.*

Also cf. *Gelli Wrgan* (Llanwynno), *Hewle Vrgan* [heol + Gwrgant] (Llantrisant) and *Caye* (cae) *Gworgan* (St.Fagan).

The founding of the *Hirwaun Ironworks* by John Mayberry of *Brecon* in 1757 on 'a certain Common, *Tyr wain Wrgan,* otherwise *Hirwain Wrgan* (CVAI.13), earmarked the birth of *Hirwaun* as an industrial town/village. The Ironworks took its name from the *Hirwaun Wrgan Common* and the town which grew around the Ironworks adopted the same *Hirwaun* name. In 1813, it consisted of around 110 tenements. (PNDH). By 1823 *Nebo Chapel* and *Bethel Chapel* had been established. (OA.vol.1.70). In 1840, it had grown to about 170 dwellings; (PNDH). The 1844 TM & TS record *Hirwaun (Iron Works), Hirwaun Common & Town* and lists tips, pastures, houses, yards, coke yard, chapel, etc.

By 1905, there were 250 dwellings,7 taverns, 8 shops, 5 mansions, coal mines, ironworks, a brickworks and the Great Western Railway station. (HPP.88/89). Also see PNDH 7.62.

The actual extent of the common appears to be roughly the pre-idustrial tract of land from the source of the *Cynon* to *the Gadlys.*

NB. "The true significance of Welsh place-names containing *gwaun* was retained in popular parlance even when they had become the names of settlements and in the Welsh language, people are always said to live 'on' (never 'in') *Hirwaun,* cf. *ar Wauncaegurwen.* Similarly with *heol* = street, road, even when it refers to the village. eg. *byw ar Heol y felin*". BFR.

pron. hee-r waa-een. hirwaun.

Sp. HIRWAUN.

Lit. meaning:- 'long moorland'.

LLANWYNNO

Llanivonno	1535	V.E. Meisg.83.
Llan wonni	1536-39	Itin.Lel.22. ibid.
Lanwyno	1549	Card.Recs.ll.277. ibid.
Lanwno	1559	Card.Recs.lV.84. ibid.
Llanwnno	1550-1600	Rep.ll.part 1.135.ibid.
Lanwynno	1578	Glam.Ants.113. ibid.
Llanwonno	1597	Card.Recs.1. 340. ibid.
Lanwonno	1666	M.M. ibid.
Llanwonnoe	1673	B.M. part 3.707. ibid.
Llanwunno	1699	Lhuyd.Paroch.iii. 9. ibid.
Llanwynno	1729	Bowen. ibid.
Lanwonnoe	1730	Plymouth. MR. PNCB.
Lanwonno	1799	Yates.
Llanwynno	1833	Colby.Meisg.83.

Welsh   Llan + Gwynno.
Llan = (parish) church
Gwynno = pers. name. (saint).
Gwynno's church.

There are over six hundred and thirty *llan* place-names in Wales, yet *Llanwynno* is the only example of a *llan* place-name in the Cynon valley. The word *llan* has an interesting etymology.

"As both English and Welsh emanate from the Indo-European languages that spread from the north of India and across Europe, there is a close relationship between the Welsh word *llan* and the English *land*.

In Welsh, the original meaning of *llan* was 'an enclosed piece of land', and this is seen today in such words as *gwinllan* (vinyard), *perllan* (orchard) and *corlan* (sheep pen).   Very soon however, the word was used for 'an enclosed cemetery', then for the church inside the cemetery and finally for the land served by that church and its vicar, (ie.) - the parish.

Very often *llan* was followed by the name of the patron saint of the parish or the founder of the church - such as *Llangadog, Llanfwrog, Llanbedr* or *Llandeilo*."

Tomos Roberts. Ditectif Geiriau. Western Mail. (trans.)

Gwynno is the patron saint of *Llanwynno* and is said to be one of the three patron saints of *Llantrisant* (along with *Illtyd* and *Tyfodwg*) as well as being one of the five saints of *Llanpumsaint (Gwyn, Gwynno, Gwynoro, Celynin* and *Ceitho).* He is also eponymous with *Maenor Gwynno* (the parish of *Vaynor*) near Merthyr Tydfil.

pron. Llan ('ll' as in Llanelli) win oh. llan<u>winn</u>o.

Sp. Llanwynno.

Literal meaning:- the parish church of Saint Gwynno.

LLETY-TURNER

Lletty'r turnor	*1799*	*Yates.*
Llety'r Tyrner	*1841*	*T.S. Llanwynno.*
Lletty Turner	*1842-50*	*PRB.Llanwynno.*
Lletty Turner	*1994*	*MAP&A. 70.*

Welsh 'llety' = lodging(s), billet, accommodation, quarters, dwelling, abode, inn; room, chamber.
    'r = the definite article, Eng. 'the'.
English 'turner' = general craft name which poss. became a pers. name.
meaning, the turner's dwelling or Turner's dwelling.

Llety. RJT. (trans.). "This element usually appears linked to pers. names and animal names, and very often as the names of small houses in remote places. When used with a pers. name it infers 'a house, small in size, enough for one, a house of an old maid or bachelor'.
eg. *Llety Adda,* (Plwyf Gwyldderwen); *Llety Brongu,* (Plwyf Llangynwyd); *Llety Ifan,* (Llyn); *Llety Lwydyn* (Cardigan) and *Llety Shiencyn,* (Cwmbach,Aberdare).
"When used in conjunction with animals, it can represent 'a place frequented by various animals, or the association of the place with the name of an animal can be a scoff at the impoverished state of the land', eg. *Llety Llyffant* (frog; toad.), *Llety'r Llygoden* (mouse), *Llety'r Frân* (crow), *Llety'r Adar* (birds), *Llety'r Filiast* (greyhound bitch)".
"*llety* is also used for a temporary dwelling for shepherds or as a summer upland dwelling like *hafod*". BFR. One of the most romantic I have observed is *Llety Gariad* (love's abode) in the parish of Llandeilo Tal-y-bont.

Turner, RJT maintains, is from the English common noun *turner,* ie. a wood turner. It is reputed that generations of wood turners lived in the forest between Taf and Cynon, making wooden dishes. see Meisg.90.
PDS describes the surname *Turner* as 'one who worked with a lathe' (making objects of wood, metal, bone, etc.) and quotes Reany as showing other occupations that could be meant, eg. 'turnspit, translator, maker of wooden wine and ale measures, jouster (one who tourneys) and even *turn hare* ie. one who could outstrip a hare. see PDS. sub nomine.

Because of the situation of the dwelling, it is likely that the *turners* were in fact lathe turners of wood.
The name survived as the Llety-turner bends, until they were recently removed from the A4059 route via the Llety-turner pass. cf. Kae Tyr Tyrnor (cae tir Turner) [Llantrisant].

pron. llet-tee ('ll' as in Llanelli) turner. llety turner.

Sp. Llety-turner.

Literal meaning:- the turner's or Turner's dwelling.

LLWYDCOED

lwytcoet(Cynon)	*c.1500*	*B.xvii. 80.MR. PNC,Bangor.*
(forest of) Lluid Coite	*1536-9*	*Leland 16. ibid.*
Lloyde Coyde	*1547*	*CR.1.456. BGA 114. ibid.*
(fforest) Llwyd Coed	*1666*	*CR.ii.93. ibid.*
Llwyt coed	*c1700*	*Par.iii.138. ibid.*
Llwydcoed	*1789*	*LTA. ibid.*
Melin Llwydgoed	*1799*	*Yates. CVAI.14.*
Llwyd-y-coed	*1833*	*OS. MR. PNC,Bangor.*
Llwyd coed	*1851*	*Census. 23.*
Llwydcoed	*1989*	*OS. Landranger 170.*

Welsh	'llwyd' + 'coed'.
llwyd =	'grey, faint (of colour, light etc); pale, pallid, wan; russet, brown; turbid, muddy (of water)'. GPC.
coed =	'forest, wood, trees'. GPC.

Generally speaking there are three colours linked to trees in Welsh place-names. ie.

DUgoed, meaning the black wood, where the trees are so numerous and closely knit, that no daylight can penetrate the leaved canopy. This is a very dark area with hardly any vegetation growth on the forest floor, leaving the floor also dark or black in colour. Later, *dugoed* possibly could also describe parts of the forest that had been burnt by charcoal burners. There are many examples of *dugoed* as field names in the 1844 TS. Aberdare.

LLWYDgoed, meaning a grey, dimly lit wood, where the trees are not as closely knit as the black wood, and so allowing a little daylight to penetrate the foliage.

GLASgoed, meaning the green wood, where the trees have been thinned, or are naturally well spaced so that there is plenty of daylight to allow a green mantled, flowered forest floor. eg. *Glasgoed,* Gwent; *Glasgoed,* Gwynedd.

Coedcae, (another place-name element linked with trees) originally referred to an enclosure that had been cleared of trees. Then it came to mean any piece of land in woods or on mountainside that had been enclosed for grazing sheep. see Meisg.14-15. also see *Parc Cae'r Felin.* eg. *Coedcae Aberaman, Coedcae Melarian* (valerian) etc.

The oldest recorded form of a *llwydgoed* place-name is in England. ie. *Letoceto* of the Antonine Itinerary (c.3rd cent.AD.). *Leto* is an earlier form of Welsh *llwyd* (cf. *lletrew, llitrew* for *llwydrew, (hoar frost)* Loughor Valley dial.) and *ceto* of Welsh *coed. Letoceto* was the early name for *Lichfield,* Staffs. *Glascote,* Wa. could also be an early form of Welsh *glasgoed.*

Llwytcoed is the local Welsh pron. of llwydcoed. ('dg' > 'tg' or 'dc'.)

pron. Ll (as in Llanelli) oo-ye-d koyd. llwydcoed

Sp. Llwydcoed.

Lit. meaning:- 'grey, dimly lit woods'.

LLWYN-ONN

Llwynon	*1767*	*PR.*	*PNDH.7.67.*
Llwynon	*1830*	*OS.*	*ibid.*
Llwynnon	*1841*	*TS.Penderyn.*	
Llwynon	*1851*	*Cens.*	*PNDH.7.67.*
Llwyn Onn	*1905*	*HPP.14.*	
Cwar Llwyn-on	*1989*	*OS.Pathfinder.1108.*	

Welsh.   'llwyn' + 'onn'.

llwyn   = 'bush, shrub, brake, thicket; copse, grove' arbour; woods, forest;...' GPC.

onn   = ash trees.

Llwynonn = (the) Ash Grove.

The original homestead was formerly where the present quarrying activity takes place. The name is preserved on the 1989 OS map as *Cwar Llwyn-on* (Llwyn-onn Quarry). A post-war housing estate in *Pontpren* also bears the *Llwyn-onn* name.

pron. ll-oo-ye non. llwyn-<u>onn</u>.

Sp. Llwyn-onn.

Lit.meaning:- ash grove.

MAERDY

Mardy	*1814*	*OS.*	*Aberdare Library.*
Maerdy Bach	*1841*	*TS.Llanwynno.*	*ibid.*
Maerdy Bach	*1842-50*	*HMH.111.*	
Maerdy	*1954*	*OS1".*	

Earlier forms are required for this apparently very old name near *Mountain Ash*. If the above forms are accurate then one may assume that it is :-

Welsh 'maerdy' = 'summer dwelling for the tending of cattle, dairy, dairy farm; farm-house; demesne, home farm, land supervisd by a reeve or steward'. GPC.
cf.'maerdre'. "..the faerdre was the personal habitat of the king or prince. In the faerdre, the serfs would live together under the authority of the land bailiff (maer biswail)." MR. TAG. (trans.).

'Another building with a similar name was the *Mardy* or *Mardy House* (sic) [built c1854.] the home of W.T.Lewis, 1837-1914, (later lord Merthyr). Subsequently it was used for a variety of purposes including local income tax offices. Aberdare Church in Wales Junior School is built in the grounds. *Mardy House* itself is now demolished and the Beeches Nursing Home stands on the site.' TE. cf. *Mardy Trip*. See *Trap*.

pron. ma eer dee. <u>maer</u>dy.

Sp. Maerdy.

Lit. meaning :- summer dwelling; land supervised by reeve or steward.

MAESCYNON

Maescynon Estate	*post WW2*	*PNDH. 7.62.*
Maescynon	*1989*	*OS. Pathfinder 1108.*
Maescynon	*1994*	*CVOH.*

Welsh   'maes' + 'Cynon.
maes = field
Cynon = river name. see Abercynon.

This post war housing estate lies within the old *Breckonshire* part of *Hirwaun.*

pron. ma-ice cun-on.   maes <u>cyn</u>on.

Sp. Maescynon.

Lit meaning:- Field (of the river) Cynon.

MEISGYN   MISKIN

Meyskin	*1233-45*	*CAD.*	*MR. PNC,Bangor.*
Meyskyn	*1268*	*CMG.*	*ibid.*
Miskyn	*1306*	*ClPM.*	*ibid.*
Kymwt Meisgyn = nn	*1400*	*R.B.B. 412.*	*Meisg.184.*
Myskyn	*1447*	*Patent.*	*MR. PNC,Bangor.*
Vro Veisgynn	*1450*	*Rep.1 Pt.2.415.*	*Meisg.184*
Misken	*1536-9*	*Leland.*	*MR. PNC,Bangor.*
Miskin	*1680*	*JAliv.*	*ibid.*
Miskin	*c1700*	*Par.*	*ibid.*
Miskin,(school).	*1862*	*HMH.p75.*	
Miskin	*1871*	*Cens.*	*Ab'dare Libry.*
Miskin	*1875*	*OS.*	*Ab'dare Libry.*

Welsh   Meis (maes) + cynn.

"Welsh, 'open field of Cyn(n)'. 'maes + pers. name Cyn(n)'. Formerly a commote [Welsh 'cwmwd', a sub-division of a cantref (a hundred)] name, and now survives in Meisgyn (Miskin) in Llantrisant and Llanwynno". MR. PNC, Bangor.

"A commote and a lordship in Glamorgan. It seems that it was a name for the district around Meisgyn manor to begin with, and it spread very early on to include the whole commote." RJT. Meisg. 184. (trans).

He also supports 'maes' + 'Cynn' = Cynn's field. (Cynn being synonymous with 'chief, leader').

Meisgyn (along with *Glyn Rhondda*) was one of the two commotes situated in the northern uplands of the cantref called *Penychen* ('ox's head', prob. totemistic).

The other commotes of the cantref were situated in the lowland of the Vale. The commote itself was split, for administrative purposes, into two areas called *Miskin Higher,* (in 1838, included the parishes of *Aberdare, Llanwynno* and the hamlet of *Rhigos*) and *Miskin Lower* [in 1838, included the parishes of *Llantrisant, Llantwit Vardre (Llanilltud Faerdre) and Pentyrch].*

The Cynon valley settlement known today as *Miskin,* located between *Penrhiwceibr* and *Mountain Ash,* was founded c.1850-62 (note date of school) and built on the lands of two farms. *Clyn Gwyn* sic. TS. 1841 & *Klyn gwynn,* 17th cent.Meisg. 434, later to become *Glyngwyn,* (also the name of a coal pit sunk on its lands) and *Ty'r Arlwydd* (the lord's house) [1842-50. PRB. HMH. 111] or *Tir Arlwydd* (lord's land/farmstead). [1841. TM. Llanwynno]. cf. Waunarlwydd, Swansea.
Arlwydd is the s.Wales form of arglwydd 'lord'.

Clun (often erroneously changed to the more familiar word *glyn* in Welsh place-names) *Gwyn* was held in demesne (used by the landowner, lord of the manor) while the lord's house/land needs no explanation, and it was fitting therefore that the old commote/lordship name should be used for the new settlement, as it would recall the administrative territory of *Miskin Higher,* while *Miskin Lower* was already represented by the *Miskin village* (along with the *Miskin Manor Hotel and Golf Course*) in the parish of *Llantrisant.* cf. *Gwaun Miskin,* (Llantrisant) and *Gorsedd Meisgyn* near Porthaethwy, Anglesey.

R.J.Thomas titled his unpublished M.A.thesis *"Astudiaeth o Enwau Lleoedd Cwmwd Meisgyn".*

pron. as Eng. 'my skin'. <u>mei</u>sgyn.
Sp. Meisgyn.

Literal meaning:- prob. Cynn's open field.

NEWTOWN

Newtown	1871	School.	HMH.75.
Newtown	1875	OS.	Ab'dare Libry.
Newtown	1881	Cens.	Ab'dare Libry.
Newtown	1910	MAP&A.44.	
Newtown	1989	OS. Landranger 170.	

English   'new' + 'town'.

Newtown was built on the land of *Troedrhiw Forest* (foot of forest hill*) & Fforest Uchaf* (upper forest*).* A school was opened in *Newtown* in 1871.

Sp. Newtown.

Lit. meaning:- new town/settlement.

NYTH-BRÂN

Griffith Morgan, Nyth bran	1700 - 1737	HMH.88. MAP&A.123.
Nyth Brane	1841	TS.Llanwynno.
Nyth Bran	1842-50	PRB.Llanwynno. HMH.115.
Nyth-bran	1989	OS Landranger 170.

Welsh   'nyth' + 'brân'.
nyth   =   nest
brân   =   'crow, rook, raven'. GPC.

Nyth-brân is legendary in Welsh folk-lore because of the exploits of the athlete who lived at the farmstead - Griffith Morgan, alias *Guto Nyth-brân.*
Guto is the hypocoristic or pet form of *Gruffydd* (as is *Gutyn*). Many Welsh names have pet forms. Here are a few examples:-
Rhys > Rhysyn; Lewis > Lewsyn, cf. Lewsyn yr Heliwr, Penderyn, (Lewis Lewis); Evan > Ianto. cf. Ianto full pelt; Iorwerth > Iori, Ioryn. cf. *Tir y Yorin*, Aberdare; Maredudd (Meredith) > Bedo; Gwenllian > Llio; Gwenllian > Gwenno; Ann > Nanno; Huw > Huwcyn; Hywel >

Hwlcyn; Margaret > Peggy, Meg; Mary, Mari > Molly; Dafydd, David >
Dai, Dei, Deio, Deicyn, Deicws; etc. see *Welsh Surnames*].

The 1841 form of *nyth brane* reflects the local dial. pron. of *brân* ie. the
'a' sounding as Welsh 'e'.
cf. Aberdâr and Aberdare; Cardiff and Kairdiff; Pwll Taf and Pwll Tave,
and the following verse:-
Ma Shani ni yn ferch fach *len*   (glân, 'clean')
Dwy foch goch a dannadd *men*   (mân, 'tiny, small')
A dwy lygad fel y *fren*   (y frân, 'the raven')
O Shani ni.
[BIBC. 58].

pron. neath brah-n.   nyth <u>brân.</u>

Sp. Nyth-brân.

Lit. meaning:- raven's nest.

PEN-Y-WAUN

Pen-y-wain	*1833*	*OS.*	*reprint.*
Pen-y-wain	*1841*	*Cens.*	*Ab'dare Libry.*
Penywain	*1897*	*school.*	*O.A.vol.1.p16.*
Pen-y-waun	*1954*	*OS1".*	
Penywaun	*1989*	*OS.*	*Landranger 170.*

Welsh   'pen' + 'y' + 'gwaun' (mutated).
pen = top; end; chief; head; mouth.
y = the.
gwaun = plain, meadow, moorland, field, moor, down.

The earliesat cottages were built on the land of *Gamlyn Isaf* farm on the
top part of *Wain Ychaf* (sic) field, hence the name *Pen-y-waun* (top end
of the *waun*). On the 1844 Tithe Map, *Wain Ychaf* is recorded as field
No. 1826 while the neighbouring cottages and gardens (occupied by
Mary David and others) are numbered 1827. The cottages also bordered
on the much larger *Hirwaun Wrgant Common* also known to Welsh-
speakers as *y waun*.

Gamlyn Isaf and *Uchaf* take their names from the land on the banks of the *Gamlyn* stream. (RJT.Meisg.82). *Gamlyn* contains two elements *cam* (crooked) and *llyn* (stream) [llyn can also mean lake] ie. crooked stream. Part of the land is also on the banks of a huge bend in the river *Cynon*.

Pen-y-waun was built mainly on the lands of *Gamlyn Isaf* while *Tre-nant* was developed on the lands of *Gamlyn Uchaf.*

pron. pen ugh waah-een. penyw<u>au</u>n.

Sp. Pen-y-waun.

Lit. meaning:- top or end of the moorland.

PENDERYN

Pennyderyn	*1291 CCRV 338. MR.PNC,Bangor.*
Penderin	*1372 CCPM.xiii.140. ibid..*
Penyderyn	*1468 BMW iii.594. RWM i.918. ibid..*
Penyderen	*1503 MLSW 120. PNDH.7.0.*
parish of Penderyn	*1515 1448.DP. ibid.*
Penyderyn	*1535 VE.402. ibid.*
parish of Pendryn(sic).	*1546 DP. ibid.*
Parish of Pennyderyn	*1547 MWBM. ibid.*
Penderyn	*1553 HPP.52. ibid.*
parish of Penderin	*1567.60.53.HPP.52. ibid.*
ym mhlwyph Penn Ederyn	*c.1600 Cymmrodor XXVII,140. ibid.*
Penyderyn	*1628 Milbonne. MR.PNC,Bangor.*
parish of Pennyderrin/Penniderrin.1650.HMB 1.6. PNDH.7.0.	
Penderin,parish of Penderrin	*1670-85 QSO ibid..*
Parish of Penderine	*1683 DP. ibid.*
Penderin	*1726 Tredegar124/615.MR.PNC,Bangor.*
Penderin	*1729 Emanuel Bowen's map of s. Wales.*
Penderyn Parish	*1748-9 WP. PNDH.7.0.*
Parish of Penderyn	*1780 DT. PNDH.7.0.*
Penderyn	*1832 OS.42. MR. PNC,Bangor.*
Plwyf Penderyn	*1905 HPP 9.*

Welsh   'pen' + 'y' + 'deryn', or 'pen' + 'aderyn'.
Pen = head, top, end.
Deryn, aderyn or y deryn = bird or the bird.

'Bird's Head'.

Here are the views of two eminent twentieth century Welsh toponymists.
'bird's head', Welsh 'pen' + 'aderyn', or 'pen' + definite article + 'deryn'.
(Melville Richards).
'Pen y deryn yw'r hen ffurfiau yn ôl i 1291, y cyfnod cynharaf'. (BLJ.).
(The bird's head are the old forms back to 1291, the earliest period).
The early recorded forms of the place-name contain the two elements *pen*
and *deryn*, dialect form of *aderyn*, with or without the definite article.
I have omitted the nineteenth century forms that deviate from the uniform
recorded forms of the previous six hundred years, eg. Pen-y-daren, Pen-
deuryn, Penderwen, as they are merely imaginative attempts at
explaining the etymology of the place-name. (see PNDH.7.0.).

The original meaning was *bird's head,* or *the bird's head.* It was
totemistic in nature, marking a boundary line or a meeting place, with
religious and tribal significances.
"Such names would have been given to sites ....where the head of the
animal was set on a pole". Cameron, *English Place Names* 122.
"these names point to a custom of setting up the head of an animal, or a
representation of it, on a pole, to mark the place for public open-air
meetings" (Bradley Memorial Volume ,101). Meisg. 274.
"An animal's head erected on a post in heathen sacrificial rites and
marking the site of a hundred meeting place, usually combined with the
name of the animal".........Smith, EPNE 236.
cf. *Gwern y pawl*, Penderyn .(swamp, meadow of the pole, post);
"probably in the sense of a boundary marker, especially as this land
bordered on the S limit of the Great Forest of Brecknock". RFPP.
PNDH. 7.60.
Also cf. poss. by association *Pwll-y-dylluan*, (the owl's pool).

English place-names in this totemistic category would be :-
Broxted, (Ess), *Broxhead,* (Ha), 'badger', Old English 'brocc'; *Eversheads,*
(Sr), 'wild boar', Old English 'eofor'; *Farcet,* (Hu), 'bull', Old English
'fearr'; *Shepshed,* (Lei), 'sheep'; *Swineshead,*(Bd), *Swinesherd,* (Wo).
'swine'; *Gateshead,* (Du) 'goat'.
Cornish:-
Pen-carrow (deer, cf. Welsh, *carw*); *Pen-kivel* (horse, cf. Welsh, *ceffyl)*;
Pen-vrane (crow, cf. Welsh, *brân, y frân).*
Scotland:-
Penicuik (cuckoo, cf. Welsh, *cog, y gog).*

Ireland:-
Kanturk (the boar's head; 'ceann' and 'tuirc') cf. *Pentyrch.*
Kincon (the hound's head; 'ceann' and 'cu');
Kinneigh (the horse's head; 'ceann-ech', cf. *Llangennech.*).

In Wales, similar activities took place.
The late Bedwyr Lewis Jones writing an article on *Pentyrch* in the Western Mail states (translated):-
'Many centuries ago, the people of a district or hundred would assemble in one particular place in order to hold meetings in the open air. In those meetings it was the custom to place the head of an animal on a pole - as a totem pole. It seems most likely that a boar's head on a pole would mark the early meeting place for each of the four Pentyrch ('s) or Bentyrch ('s) in Wales'.
Also cf. *Tir Polyn* (prob. the land of the pole) Pentyrch.
Pentyrch contains the two elements *pen* {head} and *tyrch,* genitive form of *twrch* {boar} = boar's head.
Pen Hydd (stag), *Penychen* (ox) [the cantref name of which Meisgyn was a cwmwd], *Pen yr Afr* (goat), *Pen yr Hwrdd* (ram), and *Pen March* (stallion) fall into the same totemistic category of place-names as *Pentyrch,* and (of course), *Penderyn.*

It seems likely that the name *Penderyn* for the totemistic tribal meeting place or territory, was adopted as the name of the parish and later for the name of the settlement which grew around the *Penderyn* parish church, (dedicated to St.Cynog).

Signs of early habitation:-
Early Bronze Age in Wales (circ.3,500-4,500 years ago) beakers and flints found at *Twyn bryn glas cairn, Cwm Cadlan.*
Bronze Age in Wales (c.2,500-4,500 years ago) pottery, spindle-whorl, arrowhead and flints found at *Sychbant, Penderyn.* GCBAC.

pron. pen derr-in.   pen<u>der</u>yn.

Sp. Penderyn.

Literal meaning:- Bird's head.

PENRHIW-CEIBR

Rhiw'r Kibier	*1748*	*GP.WM.*
Rhyw Kibyr	*1771-81*	*S.R.RJT.Meisg.92.*
Pen rhiw'r ceibir	*1788.S.R.1788.RJT.Meisg.92.*	
Penrhiw ciber	*1814*	*OS map.*
Penrhiw-ciber	*1833*	*Colby.RJT.Meisg.92.*
Penrhiw Ceibir	*1841*	*TS.Aberdare Library.*
Penrhiwceiber	*1842-50*	*HMH.111.*

Penrhiwceiber Station.c1863.OS1".1833.reprinted 1980.(with additions).

Welsh   'pen' + 'rhiw' + 'ceibr'.

Gwynedd Pierce has written on this place-name in Ditectif Geiriau, Western Mail. He maintains that the original form would have been *Penrhiw'rceibr* (as the 1748 form suggests), but the 'r disappeared over the years.

He re-enforces the GPC definition of *ceibr* in this place-name as that of a 'joist, beam, rafter', ie. 'a place with trees suitable for being used as roof-beams'.

Ceibr is related to the English word *caber* (from Gaelic *cabar* cf. tossing the *caber*) and the French word *chevron* (rafter, roof-beam).

The name *Pantynenbren* (roof-beam hollow) is recorded nearby in the 1841 TS.

GP also refers to the names of *Coed Ffos-ceibr* (the woods of the rafter ditch, Pendeulan, The Vale of Glamorgan) and through these woods flowed a stream called *Nant Tynplancau* (the stream of the planks small-holding [*tyn* is an abbreviated pronounciation of *tyddyn*]).

Penrhiw (top of the hill) is a common enough place-name in the Cynon Valley,

eg. *Penrhiw-angen* (top of the hill of need   ie.   poor land [BFR]), *Penrhiw-llech* (top of the hill of the flat stone), *Penrhiw Cradoc* (top of Caradog's Hill), *Penrhiw-las* (top of the green hill), *Penrhiw'r mynach* (top of the monk's hill), *Penrhiw'r porthmon* (top of the drover's hill), *Penrhiw werfa* (top of the cool, shady hill), *Penrhiw ymenyn* (top of butter hill ie. with reference to good pasture, grazing land [RJT]) etc.

Some people pronounce the place-name as 'pentre ceiber', but there is no written evidence of 'pentre' being the first element.

GP explains that the name has also been open to serious mis-spellings in the past -cibir, -ciber, -ceiber, -ceibir the most unacceptable being that of the old NCB's 'Penrikyber' Colliery. It is pleasing to note that the village infants school is called 'Penrhiwceibr Infants School'.

pron.   pen rhi-oo kie berr.   penrhiw-<u>ceibr</u>.

Sp. Penrhiw-ceibr.

Lit. meaning:- top of the joist/roof-beam/rafter hill.

PERTHCELYN

Tir y berth	*17th cent.*	*Meisg.439.*
Berthcelyn	*1841*	*TM.Llanwynno.*
Perthcelyn	*1842-50*	*PRB.HMH.111.*
Perthcelyn	*1989*	*OS. Pathfinder 1129.*
Perthgelyn	*ibid.*	

Welsh   'perth' + 'celyn'.

perth = 'hedge, thorn bush, brake, thicket, copse, coppice;
          (the) bush, countryside; jungle'. GPC.
celyn = 'holly'. plural noun. [sing. 'celynnen'].
          gelyn is the mutated form.
cf. *Perth*, Scotland; *Perthillwydion*, Denbs (*llwydion*, plural form of *llwyd*, grey); *Arberth (Narberth)* Dyfed (near, opposite to hedge, bush); *Pertholau*, Gwent (light hedge, or poss. hedge near roads); *Perth Gelyn*, Gwynedd (holly hedge); *Penberthy (perthi* pl. of *perth)* Cornwall (end of bushes, hedges) *Llwyn Celyn*, (holly bush), pub.hse. Aberdare opened 1864.

pron. perth ('e' as in Eng. 'end') kel-in.

Sp. Perthcelyn.

Lit. meaning:- holly hedge.

PLAS-DRAW

Plasdraw House	*c1870*	*APP.1.19.*
Plasdraw House	*c1900*	*ibid.*
Plasdraw House	*c1920*	*ibid.*
Plasdraw	*1979*	*Supermarket. OA.vol.7.44.*

Welsh   'plas' + 'draw'.
plas = mansion, hall, residence, abode; place, court.
draw = yonder, distant.

Plasdraw House was built by James Lewis, brother-in-law of Richard Fothergill c1870 on the lands of *Tŷ Draw*.
'Plasdraw was acquired in the 1920s by the Aberdare Cooperative Society for use as its main offices'. In 1979 it was developed as a Cooperative supermarket. [see APP.1.19].
cf. *Tir Draw* and *Tŷ Draw*. see *Tŷ Draw*.

Plas is from English *place*. It is not from Eng. *palace*. That would be Welsh *palas*.
A.H.Smith in EPNE. describes the place-name element, "place OF, place, plas ME, 'an open space in a town, an area surrounded by buildings': it is also frequent in later minor names in the senses 'a plot of ground, a residence'....
[Lat. platea 'open space']".
It is the secondary meaning of 'plot of ground, residence', that applies here. In Welsh *plas,* prob. because of the similarity with *palas,* an augmented meaning of grand house, mansion is implied.

pron. plaah-ss draa-oo (rhymes with Mau-mau,of Kenya).
plas dr<u>aw</u>.

Sp.Plas-draw.

Lit. meaning:- yonder residence (prob. implying mansion).

PONTCYNON

Pontcynon	*1750-51*	*Welsh Piety.*	*HMH.47.*
Pont Cynon	*1799*	*Yates.*	*CVAI.14.*
Pont Cynon	*1841*	*TS.Llanwynno.*	
Pontcynon	*1842-50*	*PRB.HMH.111.*	
Pont Cynon	*1954*	*OS1".*	
Pontcynon	*1989*	*OS. Pathfinder 1129.*	

Welsh   'pont' + 'Cynon.
pont = bridge, Latin 'pontem', 'pons'.
Cynon.   river name. see Abercynon.

Pontcynon takes its name from the bridge over the river Cynon circ. 1.5 miles north of *Abercynon*. The original bridge was a wooden structure. cf. *Bacon drawing* circ.1820-30, by kind permission of Aberdare Library. The present stone bridge dates from 1877. (SA.p28).
Pontcynon Farm was used as one of Gruffydd Jones Llanddowror's Circulating Schools, (note Welsh Piety 1750-51) and was also known as *Ty'r Ysgol* (the school house). [HMH. 47].
cf. *Pontargynon*, [bridge on (the) Cynon] the name on the 1814 OS map for the bridge over the river Cynon circ. 200 yards east of Aberdare, later to be known as the *Trap* bridge. (see Trap).

pron. pont kun on. pont Cynon.

Sp. Pontcynon.

Lit. meaning:- Cynon bridge.

PONTBREN-LLWYD   POMPREN-LLWYD

Pompren Llwyd	*1778-80*	*PR.1748.WP. PNDH.7.112.*
Pomprenllwyd	*1799 & 1812*	*PR. ibid.*
Pontpren Llwyd	*1799*	*Yates's map. CVAI.14.*
Pont-pren-llwyd	*1830*	*OS.*
Pontbrenllwyd	*1879*	*ERB.1871,51 Cens.PNDH.*
Pontprenllwyd	*1905*	*HPP.89.*
Pontbren Llwyd	*1905*	*OS6".*
Pontbren Llwyd	*1991*	*OS. Pathfinder 1108.*

Welsh   'pontbren' + 'llwyd'.
pontbren =   'wooden bridge, foot-bridge.' PNP.
llwyd = 1. colour, 'grey, faint (of colour) pale, pallid, wan; russet, brown;
      turbid, muddy (of water)'.
    2. 'mouldy, musty'.
    3. 'holy, blessed, pious'.
    4. 'unremarkable, insignificant, ordinary, common, uninteresting,
      not thriving'. GPC.

Pompren is the dial. form of *pontbren*, literally 'wooden bridge' but can
also mean 'footbridge'.
cf. *Cae cwm pompren, Abernant-y-groes Uchaf.* TS. 1844.

In dial. pron. "pontbren -> pon'bren -> pombren -> pompren." BFR.

D.Davies in HPP. informs us that the hamlet is very old and derived its
name from the bridge that crossed the *Cadlan* stream, on the banks of
which were a number of small thatched cottages, long since disappeared.
He tells us that the hamlet was built on the *Ysgubor Fawr* (large barn)
Estate, [eponymous with *Shoni 'Sgubor Fawr* of the Rebecca Riots] and
in 1905 it comprised 28 houses, 2 taverns (Brecon Arms, Butchers
Arms), one shop, one Baptist chapel (Siloa) and a Council School (now
Penderyn Primary). The population was 132.
Most of the 1905 hamlet can be seen today, as well as
"....a footbridge which is the case today with a modern steel structure
alongside a ford.........." R.F.Peter Powell. see PNDH.

The second element *llwyd* probably refers to the colour of the original bridge, but one cannot dismiss the fact that it might refer to the muddy waters of the stream (see 1. above) or also that it may have a historical religious significance (see 3. above) with its proximity to Penderyn parish church.

pron.   pont bren lloo-eed. ('ll' as in Llanelli). pontbren<u>llwyd</u>.

Sp.   Pontbren-llwyd.

Literal meaning:- prob. 'grey wooden bridge',
　　　　　　　　but poss. 'muddy (water) wooden bridge'.
　　　　　　　　or　 poss. 'blessed footbridge'.

ROBERTSTOWN　　　TRESALEM

Gadlys Ychaf	*1844*	*TS.Aberdare. Landowner, James ROBERTS.*
Salem	*1841*	*TMC.83.*
Robert's Town	*1853*	*Rammell.　　O.A.vol.1.p46.*
Robert's Lodge	*1861*	*Cens.　　Ab'dare Libry.*
Robertstown	*1861*	*ibid.*
Robert's town	*1875*	*OS.　　Ab'dare Libry.*
Salem Chapel	*1875*	*ibid.*
Tresalem	*19th Cent.*	*SAPN.5.*
Robertstown	*1989*	*OS. Landranger 170.*

English　　Roberts (surname) + town.

The name of the landowning family was *Roberts,* (see *Gadlys Ychaf,* 1844) and as the settlement was built on the land of *Gadlys Uchaf,* it took the name of the landowning family, and became *Robertstown.*
cf.*Carnetown,* (on land owned by the *Carne* family); *Tyntetown,* (on land owned by the *Tynte* family); *Allen's Town,*(on land owned by the *Allen* family) a lost name, near today's Caegarw. etc.
"The *Roberts* family of *Gadlys-uchaf* gave their name to the settlement developed on their land in mid century, *Robertstown.* The *Gadlys-uchaf* farmhouse stood behind *Park Grove, Trecynon* and towards *Meirion Street;*" Background Notes to 'Gardd Aberdar'.(93). D.L.Davies.

James Lewis Roberts was born in 1810, and like his father before him (*Lewis Roberts,* 1783-1844) became a doctor. He was also a magistrate, chairman of the Aberdare Board of Health as well as having business interests. He died in August 1864 (*Aberdare Times*, 20/8/1864 ed.) and lies in the family vault, inscribed with *'The Roberts's of Gadlys'*, in *St.John's* churchyard, *Aberdare*.

Tresalem, the name used by the Welsh-speaking community for the settlement comprises *tre*, (town/settlement) and *Salem*, (Hebraic word for *peace*) the name of the chapel erected there in 1841.) cf. *Caersalem & Jerusalem.*

For further details see *The Masters of the Coalfield*, by Michael Eyers.

Sp. Robertstown.

Lit. meaning:- town (of the landowning) Roberts (family).

pron. tre (as in French 'tres' eg. 'tres bien') ssaah lem. tre<u>sa</u>lem

Sp. Tresalem.   Lit. meaning:- (the) settlement (of) Salem (chapel).

Y RUGOS

The late Dr Melville Richards deeply regretted having suggested the spelling 'Y Rhigos' in Rhestr o Enwau Lleoedd/A Gazetteer of Welsh Place-Names and strongly advocated 'Y Rugos'. He accepted 'Ricos' as the local dialect pronounciation. see his article on 'Y Rugos' (Iaith a Llen.8-9).

Rugoys	*1314*	*CIPMV. MR.*
Rigois,Rigos	*1536-9*	*Leland. MR.*
Rygoes (Rhydgroes).	*16th cent.*	*Par iii. 120.MR.*
Rigos	*1666*	*CFL Morg. MR.*
Rhigoes	*1789*	*LTA. MR.*
Rhygos	*1793*	*LTA. MR.*
Rhy-goes	*1799*	*Yates's map. CVAI 14.*
Rhydgroes	*1833*	*OS. MR.*
Rhigos	*1851*	*census. MR.*
Cefn Rhigos	*1954*	*OSI ".*
Rhigos Halt	*1954*	*OSI ".*

Welsh   'y' + 'grugos', ['grug (heather) + -os', mutated to 'y rugos' dial. pron. 'ricos'].

the place of heather; the heath.

Rhydgroes is to be ignored as it is merely an effort at 'correcting' the name.
Cefn Rhigos (rugos) means the ridge of the place of heather.
Rhigos Halt refers to the old railway line.

Many Welsh place-names follow this pattern of having the name of a tree or type of vegetation plus the old collective suffix -os.
eg. *Y Wernos, gwernos* (alder). cf. *Y Wernos Deg,* Beddgelert; *Onnos*(ash), eg. *Yr Onnos, Ystradfellte*; *rhedynos* (fern); *helygos* (willow). cf. *Lygos, Cwm Tawe*; *bedwos* (birch). cf. *Bedwas; panos* *(*cotton grass). cf. *Trebanos,* Cwm Tawe; *tafol* (docks). cf. *Gelli Dafolos* (dial. dafolws), Penderyn; *dreinos* (brambles). cf. *Ton Drunoss,* Plymouth Surveys. etc.

MR. identifies other places in Wales with *grugos* as a place-name element, eg. *Y Rugos,* Llandinam; *Grugos,* Tre-lech a'r Betws; *Grugos,* Llandyfalle; *Grugos,* Talgarth; *Grugos,* Llanllwchaearn; *Cefn-Grugos,* Llannarth; *Clun y rugos,* (Glyn Rhigos on recent maps) Dulais, Neath; *Erw Grugos,* Pen-bre; *Ton(y)grugos,* Tonna; *Pantygrugos,* Llannarth; and *Twyn y Rugos,* Llangynidr (Twyn y Rhicos).

pron. ugh ree goss. y <u>ru</u>gos. local pron. <u>rick</u>oss.

Sp. Y Rugos.

Literal meaning :- the place of heather.

TRAP

Trap	*1820*	*Parish vestry minute.TE.*
Trap	*1841*	*census. Aberdare Library.*
Trap Bridge	*1842*	*OA.vol.1.20.*
Trap Meadow	*1844*	*Ty Draw,1175. TS.Aberdare.*
trap,little field	*1844.prt.Blaenant.1274. TS.Aberdare.*	
Trap Rd & Row.	*1871*	*census. Aberdare Library.*
Trap Row	*1875*	*OS map. Aberdare Library.*
Trap Surgery	*1914*	*APP.2.61.*
Trap Lane	*1995*	*MSP.Aberdare.*

English   'trap'.

As it is English and is not recorded before 1820, we can assume that the word is linked with the early industrialisation of the valley. It is unlikely that it was linked with the trapping of animals or fish, for then, it would prob. have been pre-industrial and more likely therefore to have been Welsh ['magl', 'cored' etc].

TE informs me that the tramroad (1810-12) intersecting the parish road was the exact location of the Trap. Another meaning of *trap* is a step. The tram road intersection could have formed a step on the old parish road.

A word closely related to *trap* is *trip*. This is to be found in *Forge Trip, Abernant; Gadlys Trip, Aberdare* and *Maerdy Trip, Aberdare*. IW in Ell. P.22 defines *trip* as English 'step', from the same root as *trap,* with '*trip* to be found as a common element in the names of hills, hillsides, ascents and slopes'. (trans.).

In a court case in 1853, the truck shop in Abernant was wittily referred to as a *trap*. O.A. vol v.

A 'trap' often applies to public houses. There was a *Star and Railway Inn* at 1, Abernant Road, Aberdare [opened 1835, IHBHAD.] and a *White Hart Inn* at 4, Abernant Road, Aberdare, [opened 1865, IHBHAD.]. Although too recent to have been the original, the name 'trap' could have been transferred to these public houses (poss. '*tap-house*' > '*trap-house*' . GP.).

The Pontargynon bridge (Aberdare) of the 1814 OS map had, by 1842 become known as the *Trap Bridge.*

The name was also applied to *Trap Surgery* and more recently to *Trap Lane.*

It is possible that the *Trap* name started with the tramroad intersection, then it transferred to the Truck shop, the bridge and later, by popular etymology, probably jocular, to the public houses and then to the surgery. It remains with us today as *Trap Lane.*

The name was given to the area or district around the original 'trap'.

Sp. Trap.   Lit. meaning:- origin uncertain.

TREBANOG

Trebanog	*1560*	*55 HPP.52. PNDH.7.128.2.*
Trebannog	*1768*	*48 DP. ibid.*
Trebannog Fawr	*1794*	*PR. ibid.*
Trebannog Fawr	*1841*	*TS.Penderyn.*
Trebanog	*1905*	*HPP.17.*
Trebanog	*1954*	*OS1".*

also, Trebanog-Fach, Trebanog-Ganol, Melin Trebanog, Trebanog-Isaf and Trenanog-Uchaf. [see PNDH for dates and forms].

Welsh   'tre' + 'panog' or 'bannog'.

tre   = farm, homestead, dwelling place.

panog   =   'wooly material, fluffy plants, cotton grass'; (trans.). 'mullein'. GPC. or

bannog 1. =   'high, elevated; exalted, famous, conspicuous, notable, distinctive'. GPC.

bannog 2. = 'turreted, battlemented'. GPC.

bannog 3. = 'horned'.

or as a noun, bannog = name of a mountain in Scotland, 'Bannauc', cf. Bannockburn.

Trebannog probably takes its name from the topography of the area ie. the farm on high or elevated land.

The secondary meaning of exalted, famous, conspicuous, notable might also be applicable for *Trebanog* was obviously a prestigious name.

Six farmsteads have adopted it, from the original *Trebanog*, 1560, possibly via the Welsh inheritance system of gavelkind, which divided the large estate into smaller units, each keeping the name of the 'parent' residence.   The original *Trebanog* would indeed have been a large holding and worthy of the *'bannog 1'* meaning 'exalted, prestigious, famous'.

It is also possible however, that the second element is 'pan' + 'og' and refers to the vegetation of the site, ie. covered in cotton grass or mullein. This is a common occurrence in place-names, eg. *brwynog*, of rushes; *celynnog*, of holly; *coediog,* wooded; *dreiniog,* thorny; *haiddog*, of barley [Haydock, Manchester], etc.

cf.Trebanos,Cwm Tawe.

A fourth possibility is [as suggested by MR. (TAG 63)] that the second element is linked to *pandy* and *pannau* [as in *Trebandy* and *Trebannau*] and refers to a place where wool or cloth was treated, ie. fulling mill.

Melin Trebanog adds weight to this theory, ie. a fulling mill, which one might expect to find, in this sheep rearing region.

Until further documentary evidence is forthcoming, one must remain undecided re. the second element *bannog* or *panog*.

cf. *Trebanog*, Rhondda Fawr.

pron. tre (as in French 'tres') ban nog. tre<u>ban</u>og.

Sp. Trebanog.

Lit. meaning:- prob. highland, elevated farm,
          but poss. fulling farm,
      or   prestigious farm,
      or   cotton grass farm.

TRECYNON

Trecynon	*c1850-60?*	*Local eisteddfod competition. SAPN,p5.*	
Trecynon Society	*1865*	*Abdre.Coop.Soc. OA.vol.7. 31.*	
Trecynon	*1871*	*Cens.*	*Ab'dare Libry.*
Tre-Cynon	*1875*	*OS.*	*Ab'dare Libry.*
Trecynon	*1885*	*Hist.Sktch.*	*OA.vol.1.60.*

Welsh   'tre(f)' + 'Cynon'.

'tref' = "originally 'house, dwelling-place, homestead', including the land held with the homestead; it developed the sense 'hamlet, village' probably at first to indicate 'the group of villein homesteads clustered together for the purpose of common cultivation of the surrounding land' (HW 295) and much later the modern sense 'town'. .PNDPH.347.
It also corresponds to English 'tun'.

Cynon.   river name. see Abercynon.

The *tre* in *Trecynon* has the latest meaning of 'town'. *Trecynon* was submitted in an eisteddfod competition, in the 1850s, to devise an appropriate name for the mid 19th century constructed 'suburb', and was later accepted as the official appellation. cf. 1865 name. This settlement was sited predominantly on the lands of two farms, namely *Tir Iorin* (pet form of Iorwerth,Yorath. cf. Iorin.) and *Gadlys Uchaf* (see 'gadlys').

Later in the century, land was granted and released from the *Hirwaun Common* by the Enclosure Commissioners for the laying out of the cemetery (1860) and the Park (1869). The Primary school with *Trecynon* as its catchment area is called *'Ysgol-y-Comin'* as it also was constructed on land acquired from *Hirwaun Common*.

cf. *Tregynon* near Newtown,Powys.

Previously the earlier settlement had been known as *Heol y felin* [1751] (the mill road), as it had established itself along the road that lead to *Melin Llwydcoed* (Yates1799). cf. with today's 'Mill Street' and 'Mill House'.

BFR states that the older generation of Welsh-speakers always referred to living 'ar Heol y Felin'- ie. the area not the street.

In south Wales, the dial.pron. of 'heol' is 'hewl'.

Hen-Dy-Cwrdd, (1751) alias The Old Meeting House is also identified on Yates's map of 1799.

Other municipal 'tre' names created at a later date were :-

Trefelin, Tre-nant, Treniol, Tre-waun and *Tre-ivor.* see SAPN. p5.

For *Tresalem* see *Robertstown*.

"It is pleasing to note that the local authority has remembered and paid tribute to its linguistic heritage by using Welsh place-names for these settlements. It is to be commended for adopting this policy and it is hoped that this enlightened strategy will continue." BFR.

pron. tre (as in French 'tres') kun non. Tre<u>cyn</u>on

Sp. Trecynon.

Literal meaning:- Cynon town.

TREGIBBON   TREGIBWN

Tregibon	*1814*	*OS.*	*Aberdare Library.*
Tregibbon	*1841*	*Cens.*	*Aberdare Library.*
Tre Gibbon	*1844*	*TS.Aberdare.[Incld.Corner House Pub.Hse.]*	
Tre-Gibbon	*1954*	*OS1".*	
Tre Gibbon	*1989*	*OS.Landranger 160.*	

Welsh + Eng.   'tre' + 'Gibbon' (pers. name).
tre   = town, etc.
Gibbon = Eng. pers. name.
'Gibbon' a dim. of 'Gibb', itself a dim. of 'Gilbert'. PDS.

"the houses at *Tre-Gibbon*, which were built to accommadate the workers of the Aberdare Iron works at Llwydcoed, date from c.1801 and were erected by Thomas Jenkin alias Gibbon (probably Thomas ap Shencin ap Gibbon) of Fforchaman Farm who had acquired Tir Evan Shone Rees by 1800." APP vol 2. p6.

Welsh-speaking local pron. is Tregibwn.

Sp. Tregibbon. Tregibwn.

Lit. meaning:- Gibbon's town.

91

TRE-NANT

Tre nant   c1935   TE.BFR.
Tre-Nant   1991   OS.Pathfinder 1108.
Tre-nant   1994   CVOH.

Welsh.   'tre' + 'nant'.

tre (f)   =   town, home, house, dwelling place, homestead; hamlet, village.
nant   =   stream,brook.

'Tre nant was built in the mid 1930s for the inhabitants of the condemned houses in Trap Row, Cobbler's Row (Lower Abernant) and possibly Long Row (opposite Richmond Tce.).   There is a tiny stream here (in Trenant), but at the time the received wisdom was that it was called Trenant because the people came from Abernant (in the broadest sense).'
TE.
In the 1853 Rammell Report on the state of sanitary conditions in the parish of Aberdare, *Cobbler's Row* is described as "a cluster of houses without backdoors, back windows or back openings of any kind".
Eighty years later the houses were condemned and the inhabitants re-settled in *Tre-nant*.

Sp. Tre-nant.

Lit. meaning:- hamlet (near the) brook.

TŶ - DRAW

Ty Draw	1800	T.Dadford letter. TE.
Ty Draw	1821	SAPN.
Tyr Draw	1823	ibid.
Ty Draw	1832	ibid.
Tir Draw	1844	TS.Aberdare.
Ty Draw	1844	ibid.
Ty Draw	1900	OS.25" Aberdare.
Ty Draw Place	1900	ibid.

Welsh   'ty' + 'draw', 'traw'.
tŷ   =   house
draw =   yonder, there, beyond; furthest.

There is an interplay of *tŷ* and *tir* in the recorded form of this place-name. This is not uncommon, because of the similarity in sound and meaning.
Tir (land) is virtually synonymous with *tŷ* (house) in the sense that the house is situated on the land of that name. see *Aber-gwawr*.
There is also the Welsh idiom *tu draw* meaning beyond, on the other side, but this *tu* is unlikely to be the first element of this place-name.

Draw has the same meaning as *hwnt* which is also found in Cynon valley place-names. eg. *Caia Hwnt* (yonder fields); *Cwm Hwnt* (yonder valley) Y Rugos is situated near *Ty draw* Farm, Y Rugos. Also cf. *Ty-draw* (Llantrisant) and *Yonder Field* (prob. a trans. of Cae-draw) [St.Fagan].
'These names derived their meanings from a particular perspective ie. yonder, distant from the farm (as caia hwnt) or some other settlement; Ty-draw presumably from Aberdare village ie. across the river Cynon.' BFR.

Plas-draw was built on the lands of *Tŷ draw*. see *Plas-draw*.

Pron.   tee drah-oo.

Sp. Tŷ-draw.

Lit. meaning:- Yonder house.

TŶ-FRY

Tyr bryd	*1759*	*SAPN.21.*
Tyr Fryd	*1766*	*ibid.*
Tyr Vryd Farm	*1832(or Rhiwmenich). ibid.*	
Cae'r ty Ychaf	*1844*	*TM. Ynys Llwyd, Field no.2033.*
Tir Fry	*1854*	*SAPN.21.*
Tir Fry	*1871*	*cens. Aberdare Library.*
Ty Fry Farm	*1875*	*OS. Aberdare Library.*
Ty Fry	*1992*	*CVOH. map.*

Welsh   'ty' + 'bry'.
tŷ   = house.
fry   = (mutated form of 'bry') 'above, aloft, on high'. GPC.

tŷ fry = upper house, top house.

The post-war *Tŷ Fry* housing estate was built on part of the land of *Ty Fry* farm (note OS map of 1885). The site is identified as corresponding to field no. 2033 on the 1844 Tithe map and schedules. The field was called *Cae'r Ty Ychaf* (field of the upper house, or the upper 'house-field'), and it was part of *Ynyslwyd* farm.
Ty uchaf has the same meaning as *Tŷ Fry*.

However, the second element in the earlier forms *Tir bryd* and *Tir Fryd*, *Tyr Vryd* is obscure and *Tŷ Fry* could have emerged from popular etymology.
Bryd could poss. be linked with *breuder*, meaning brittle or frail land, but further conclusive evidence is needed.

Tir and *tŷ* are often confused an substituted for each other in the records (as above).

Rhiwmenich, 1832 comprises two elements, *rhiw* (hill) and either *mynach* (monk) or the plural form *mynaich* (monks) = Monk's or Monks' Hill. cf. today's Monk Street.
Popular etymology links the hill with the route that monks of the middle ages would have taken on their pilgrimages to the famous shrine of Mary at Penrhys.

pron. tee vree.

Sp. Tŷ-fry.

Lit. meaning:- 'upper, top house'.

TYNTETOWN

Ynysboeth Ucha   *1842-50 HMH.111. [landowner,**C.K.Tynte**,Esq.]*
Tynetown   *1896-06 Glam XIX SW.= 31/09. MR. PNC,Bangor.*
Mathewstown.(the Tynte).c1905   MAP&A.41.
Tynetetown   *1954   OS1".*
Tynetetown   *1964   HMH.102.[after Tynte family,landowners]*
Tynetetown   *1989   OS.Landranger 170.*
Tynetown   *1995   MSP.Mountain Ash.*

English   'Tynte' + 'town'.

Tynte = surname of landowning family.
          eg. C.K.Tynte. [see PRB. 1842-50.]
town = a populous place.

The *Tynte* family had links with *Began (prob. beacon)* near *Llanedeyrn*
(the church of Edern < Lat. eternus) and also *Cefn Mabli (Mabilia,
Mabel's mountain ridge).*
Charles Kemys Tynte was born in 1822 and died in 1891. He was a
magistrate and deputy lieutenant for the counties of Somerset and
Monmouthshire. He married three times.
He was succeeded by his son from the first marriage, Halswell·Milborne
Kemys-Tynte, 1852-1899, and it was during the later part of his life that
Tyntetown was built. *Halswell St. Milborne St. Wash St.* and *Bagot St.*
are all named after members of the Tynte family. [see TMC.114-115.]

The name Tynte is obscure, prob.of Anglo-Norman descent.

In PRB 1842-50, C.K. Tynte is recorded as owner of :-
Troedfeddi, Gelliwrgan, Gilfachyrhydd, Ynysboeth Ucha, Ffynondwym,
and *Llwynperdid.*

pron. tint town.

Sp. Tyntetown.

Lit. meaning:- town (built on) Tynte ('s land).

GWERFA   Y WERFA

Tir Werva	16th.cent.	BFR. SAPN. 24.
Tire Werva	1638	S.M. 1638. Meisg.81.
Tyr y werva	1788	ibid.
Wyrfa	1833	Colby. Meisg.81.
Werfa	1844	TS.Aberdare.
Werfa Colliery sunk	1845	APP.vol.1. 56.
Y Werfa	1854	BFR. SAPN.24.
Twyn y Werfa	1854	ibid.
Werfa Colliery closed	1908	APP.vol.1. 56.
Werfa Colliery(dis).	1989	OS Pathfinder 1109.
Werfa House	1989	ibid.
Twyn y Werfa	1989	ibid.

Welsh   'gwerfa', 'y werfa'.

IW informs us that *gwerfa* is composed of two elements *go-oer* + *fa* and signifies a cool place, as Dafydd ap Gwilym had used *go-oer* with the same meaning as the English 'cool'; *-fa* (ma) equates with *man,* a place, as in *disgwylfa* (place of observation), *arosfa* (stopping place), *porfa* (place for grazing), *rhodfa* (walking place), *mynedfa* (place of entry, exit), *gorffwysfa* (resting place), *cynhesfa* (a warm place), *sgwrfa (a scouring place)* etc.
Gwerfa is used in Glamorgan for a shady nook where cattle or sheep may shelter from the heat of the sun.
BFR defines *gwerfa* as 'a cool place, sheltered from the sun, shade for cattle and sheep'.
'go-oerfa - cool place, the shade', GPC.
eg.
   'Mae'r da yn dala *gwerfa*' (Bridgend area).ibid.
   [the cattle ar holding a shady place].
   'Dewch yma i'r *wyrfa*' (Mynydd Islwyn). ibid.
   [come here to the cool place].

96

The use of the definite article (Eng. 'the') causes a soft mutation, therefore *gwerfa* becomes *y werfa*. Often the definite article is abandoned in place-names, hence *werfa* (as in 1788,1844, etc.). *Wyrfa* was the local dial, pronounciation. also NB. Mynydd Islwyn, above.

Other examples of *y werfa* are:-
Y Werfa ddu, Llantrisant; *Y Werfa*, Henllan, Dyfed; *Werfa Dâr*, GPC. *Rhiw y Werfa*, Hirwaun, 1792, GOP, WM and *Rhydywerfa*, Llandeilo-tal-y-bont TS 1844.
John Nixon started the *Werfa Colliery* in 1845. It closed in 1908.

Twyn y Werfa signifies the 'hillock, knoll' of the *Werfa*.

pron. ugh wair (rolled 'r') va.

Sp. Y Werfa.

Literal meaning:- 'the cool, shady place'.

YNYS-Y-BŴL

Ynys y Bool	1738-9	*Meisg.97.*
Ynis y Bwl	1799	*Yates. CVAI.14.*
Ynnis-y-bool	1813	*NLWJ.ix.38. MR.PNC,Bangor.*
Ynys y bwl	1814	*OS. Aberdare Library.*
Ynysybwl.Pub.Hs.	1842-50	*HMH.109.*
Ynysybwl		1888 (Gelwir ef yn Saesneg'Bowling Green').
		GlP 4.14.
Ynysybwl	1989	*OS.Pathfinder 1129.*

Welsh   'ynys' + 'y' + 'bwl'.
ynys   =   river meadow.
y   =   the.
bŵl   =   from ME 'boule', bowl, ball, round object, knob. cf. Scots. *bool*.

The third element *bŵl* is not as uncommon as it would seem. It is used, either in a topographical sense of a bowl shaped valley or a round hill or hillock, or as the name of a river meadow used for a game played with a ball or bowl.

There is evidence that the game of boules or bowls was played in the county as a 15th cent. Glamorgan bard wrote:-
"Tawlu *bwl* bach pwy sy ffelach". GPC. (throwing a small boule, who is more skillful). Incidentally *tawlu* (> *twlu*) is the Gwentian dial. form of *taflu*. It is possible that *Ynys-y-bwl* was the venue for games of boules or bowls.
On the other hand the place-name could be topographical.
cf. *Waun bwl*, Pembs; *Berth y Bwl*, Flint. & *Bryn Bwl*, Cards.

pron. un niss ugh bool. ynysy<u>bwl</u>.

Sp. Ynys-y-bwl.

Lit.meaning:- the bowl (or bowling) river meadow.

YNYS-BOETH

Ynys boeth issa	*1632-3*	*CFL. GLA. MR. PNC,Bangor.*
Ynysboeth yssa,ycha	*1636*	*GRO. D/DRT. ibid.*
ynis both issa,ycha	*1782*	*LTA. ibid.*
Ynysboeth-isaf,uchaf	*1833*	*OS. ibid.*
Ynis Both Isha	*1841*	*T.S.Llanwynno. Aberdare Library.*
Ynis Both Ucha	*1841*	*ibid.*
Ynysboeth Isha	*1842-50*	*PRB.Llanwynno. HMH.*
Ynysboeth Ucha	*1842-50*	*ibid.*
Ynys-boeth	*1954*	*OSM1".*
Ynysboeth	*1989*	*OS. Pathfinder 1129.*

Welsh 'ynys' + 'poeth'.
ynys =   1. 'meadow, pasture on the banks of a river or stream; river meadow'.
           2. 'island'.
poeth = hot; burnt; pungent; inflamed.

Ynys can be confusing in place-names because the immediate reaction of a Welsh speaker when asked the meaning of *ynys*, invariably is to say 'island'. (cf. Ynyswendraeth).   This is true of place-names on the coastline or on river estuaries, but the great majority of inland place-names containing the element *ynys* refer to a meadow or pasture near water, ie. a river meadow, eg.
Ynys Cynon (Cynon river meadow); *Ynys Daf* (Taf river meadow); *Yr*

Ynys (the river meadow; *Ynys fain* (narrow river meadow); *Ynys Fawr (large river meadow) and Ynyslwyd* (s.n.) all in the Cynon Valley.

Place-names around the sea shore containing this element and meaning 'island' include:- *Ynys Byr* [Caldey Island. (*Byr* < pers. name *Pyr*. cf. *Maenor Byr,* Manorbier)]; *Ynys Enlli* (Bardsey Island); *Ynys Fôn* (Anglesey), etc.

The 's' in *Sketty* (Swansea) is all that remains of this element in its present form. Originally however it was *Ynys Ceti* (Ceti's island, cf. *Cilgeti* [Pembs], Ceti's retreat].

This Celtic place-name element can also be found in the form of:-
inis, eg. Innisfallen; *inish,* eg. Innishannon; *enis,* eg. Enniskillen and *inch*, eg. Inchkeith.

Poeth meaning hot, burnt, could refer to a sunny river meadow, usually with a thin layer of soil, covering rock or stone, that bakes and retains the sun's heat, or it could refer to some industrial activity that involved heat. eg charcoal burning.

see PNDH, 5.18. *Derwen-Boeth.*

cf. *Cae Poeth,* Dyffryn Darc; *Tre-boeth*, Swansea & Llantrisant (see Meisg. 213) & *Coed-poeth,* Clwyd.

Poth, both is the local pronounciation of *poeth, boeth.*

  cf. *hewl* for *heol, ca* for *cae, caia* for *caeau, worlodd, werlod, wyrlod* for *gweirglodd, llwye* for *llwyau, cenol* for *canol, bech* for *bach, bidy* for *beudy, tyla* for *tyle, gotre* for *godre, nuadd* for *neuadd, defyd* for *defaid, blan* for *blaen, harn* for *haearn, gelynan* for *gelynen, fallan* for *afallen, gola* for *golau, Hwel* for *Hywel* ,etc.

For more examples, see 'Blas ar Iaith Blaenau'r Cymoedd', Mary William. Llyfrau Llafar Gwlad.

pron. un(rhymes with gun) niss bo-eeth. Ynysboeth.

Sp.Ynys-boeth.

Literal meanig:- 'hot, burnt river meadow'.

YNYSCYNON

ynys kynon	*1632*	*SAPN.24.*
ynys kinon	*1656*	*ibid.*
Tir Ynys Cynon	*1666*	*ibid.*
Ynis Kynon	*1799*	*Yates. CVAI.14.*
Ynysgynon	*1814*	*OS map. Aberdare Library.*
Ynyscynon	*1833*	*OS1".*
Ynys Cynon	*1844*	*TS.Aberdare.*
Ynyscynon Colliery	*c1845*	*APP.1.41a.*
Ynyscynon House	*c1850*	*APP.1.41a.*
Ynyscynon Shop	*1869*	*IHBHAD.sn.*
Ynyscynon Street	*1995*	*MSP.Aberdare.*

Welsh   'ynys' + 'Cynon'.
ynys =   river meadow.
Cynon =   river name.[see Abercynon].

Ynyscynon (Cynon river meadow) the farm name dates back to 1632 and poss. earlier. In 1975 *Ynyscynon Farm* became *The Golden Post* public house. *Ynyscynon House* stands on the bank of *Nant y geugarn* (stream of the deep cairn) on the bend of the road out of Cwmbach towards Aberdare and was the home of coalowner David Williams, bardic name, *Alaw Goch* (red air/tune/music) [*Trealaw*, Rhondda is named after him. He bought land and sank a coalpit there c1853]. He started *Ynyscynon Colliery* c1845. *Ynyscynon Shop* closed in 1869. *Ynyscynon Street* connects Well Place and Pinecroft Avenue.

pron. un(rhymes with Eng. 'gun') niss <u>kyn</u> non. ynys<u>cyn</u>on.

Sp. Ynyscynon.

Lit. meaning:- Cynon river meadow.

YNYS-LWYD

Ynyslwyd.(copy).	*1745PR.(copied from original,prob.mod.sp.).Abd.Lib.*	
ynis llwyd	*1759 1766*	*SAPN.*
Ynyslwyd	*1841*	*cens. Aberdare Library.*
Ynys Llwyd	*1844*	*TS.Aberdare.*
Ynislwyd Inn	*1861*	*IHBHAD.sn.*
Ynyslwyd	*1862-67*	*School.HMH.74.*
Ynyslwyd School	*1875*	*Hist.of Blaengwr Schls.OA.vol.iii?.127.*
Ynysllwyd Farm.	*1989*	*OS. Pathfinder.1109.*

Welsh   'ynys' + 'llwyd' or 'Llwyd'.
ynys = river meadow.
llwyd = grey, pale, brown; holy. GM. see Llwydcoed.
Llwyd = surname. cf. Tir Feurig Llwyd. [tir Veyryg llwyd].

The second element is not as straightforward as it appears. It could be *llwyd* (russet, brown) the colour of the river meadow. [*llwyd* can vary in colour from grey, faint, pale to russet or brown. It can also refer to poor land as well as muddy water.]
It might on the other hand, be *Llwyd*, the surname of the original owner. (see above).

pron. un niss loo-eed. ynys<u>lwyd.</u>

Sp.Ynys-lwyd.

Lit. meaning:-   prob. russet/brown river meadow, or poor,infertile river meadow, or poss. (the surname) Llwyd's river meadow.

YNYSWENDRAETH

Ynis bendorth	*1570*	*TR.*	*BBC,Difyrru'r Dydd.*
Ynyswendorth	*1767*	*PR.*	*PNDH.7.143.*
Ynyswaendorth	*1770*	*ibid.*	
Ynyswaindorth	*1790*	*ibid.*	
Ynyswendorth	*c1797*	*HB iv.72. PNDH.7.143.*	
Yniswendorth	*1808*	*ibid.*	
Ynyswendorth	*1830*	*OS.*	
Yniswenddor	*1841*	*TS.Penderyn.*	
Yniswen-Porth	*1841*	*cens.*	*PNDH.7.143.*
Yniswendrath	*1854*	*SRB.*	*ibid.*
Yniswendraeth	*1871*	*cens.*	*ibid.*
Yniswendraeth	*1879*	*ERB.*	*ibid.*
Ynyswerndraeth	*1905*	*HPP.13.*	
Ynyswendraeth	*1926*	*Kelly.*	*PNDH.7.143.*
Ynyswendraeth	*1989*	*OS.Pathfinder 1108.*	

Welsh   'ynys' + 'pen' + 'torth'
ynys = river meadow; island.
pen   = top, end, hill, head, height.
torth = a loaf.

Ynys bendorth, the 1570 name is by far the earliest recorded form of this *Penderyn* farm name, and I am grateful to Tomos Roberts on BBC Radio Cymru's Difyrru'r Dydd programme for this early form.
The first element *ynys* has been recorded consistently over the centuries, and refers to a river meadow [as is the norm for inland 'ynys' names].
The second and third elements have varied considerably since 1570. *ben* [mutated form of *pen*] has changed, prob. through a series of mutations b > f > w (see Ystradfellte) or by popular etymology to *waun* [mutated form of *gwaun,* 'moorland,meadow'] and *wen* [mutated form of *gwen,* 'white'].
The original *ben* means 'hill', or 'top' or 'end of'.
The third element has also varied in form, from *torth* to *ddor, porth* and *traeth.* [for explanations on the variations, see PNDH. 7.143.].
Torth (loaf) is the original, and refers to the shape of the hill. ie.in the shape of a loaf.
cf. *Mesur-y-dorth,* Pembs; *Y Dorth-wen,* N.Wales?. (TR.); *White Bread,* Chesh. (EFN.); *Sugar Loaf,* Gwent; *Sugar Hill,* Lim. & *Sugarloaf Mountain*, Cork.

The original form, *Ynysbendorth,* means 'loaf (shaped) hill (of the) river meadow'.

pron. originally, un niss ben dorth. ynys<u>ben</u>dorth.
today, un niss wen drah-eeth. ynys<u>wen</u>draeth.

Sp.Ynyswendraeth, from Ynyswendorth, from YNYSBENDORTH.

[Ynyswendraeth (white beach island) has prob. resulted in pop. etymology due largely to the misinterpretation of *ynys* as 'island' instead of *ynys* 'river meadow'].

Lit. meaning :- Loaf hill river meadow.

YSGUBOR-WEN

Ysgubor Wen	*1844*	*TS.*
Ysgubor wen	*1854*	*SAPN.24.*
Ysguborwen Level	*1850*	*APP.55.*
Ysguborwen Hotel	*1976*	*IHBHAD.sn.*
Ysgubor-wen House	*1989*	*OS.1989 Pathfinder 1109.*
Ysgubor-wen Farm	*1989*	*ibid.*
Ysguborwen Nursing Home	*1990*	*visited.*

Welsh   'ysgubor' + 'gwen' (mutated to 'wen').

ysgubor   =   barn; building in which grain, hay etc. is stored.
              dial. form 'sgibor, sgipor', plural 'ysguboriau', dial. 'sgibora'.
              Cornish 'sciber', prob. > Eng. 'skipper' (barn, outbuilding).
gwen   =   white. Feminine form of 'gwyn'.

It acquired its name apparently as the land contained a whitewashed barn.
The word *ysgubor* appears quite often in Cynon valley place-names, as one would expect in the pre-industrial agricultural community.   e.g. *Ysgubor-Fawr* (large barn), Penderyn; *Coed Ysgubor* (barn woods), Aberamman Ychaf, TS, 356; *Cae Ysgubor* (barn field), Tir Draw, TS, 1147 and general; *Waun Ysgubor* (barn meadow), Tir Llaethdy, TS. 126; etc.

In 1844 *Ysgubor-wen* was part of the estate of landowner Robert Henry Clive.

In 1850 the *Ysgubor-wen* coal level was opened by Samuel Thomas, and in 1856 his son David Alfred Thomas, later to become Viscount Rhondda, was born in *Ysguborwen House*.

In the 1970s it became a hotel, locally called 'the skip' and in the late 1980s it was transformed into a nursing home.

pron. ugh skee bor wen. ysgubor wen.

Sp. Ysgubor-wen.

Lit. meaning:- white barn.

YSTRADFELLTE

Melltou	*c1150*	*Lib.Land.134.*	*EANC.178.*
Stratmeltin (prob.)	*1230*	*Brych xiii,88.*	*PNDH, 12.0.*
Ystradfellte	*14cent*	*SWB.*	*ibid.*
Ystrad vellte	*1502*	*MWBM,587.*	*ibid.*
Estrodwelthy	*1503*	*MLSW,33, 123.*	*ibid.*
Stradvellte	*1531*	*MWBM,589.*	*ibid.*
Ystradveltye	*1547*	*MWBM,610.*	*ibid.*
Istradveltie	*1601*	*CARW,208.*	*ibid.*
Strodwelty	*1650*	*GFB, 13.*	*ibid.*
Ystradfellte	*1670*	*HB iv 75.*	*ibid.*
Ystradfellte	*1819*	*GFB xxxix*	*ibid.*
Ystradvelltey	*1851*	*R Cens 236*	*ibid.*
Ystradfellte	*1886*	*ERB, 1842.TM.*	*ibid.*
Ystradfellte	*1905*	*HPP.91.*	
Ystradfellte	*1967*	*OSI".*	

Welsh   ystrad + Mellte, (mutated to 'Fellte'.)

ystrad = 'level place, valley bottom, river valley.' IW.

In Ell. 29, IW. states that *ystrad* is not borrowed from Lat. *strata (a paved road)*. Welsh *ystrad* and Lat. *strata* are descended from an older tongue, mother to both *Latin* and *Celtic*.

"The Welshman did not borrow it, but acquired it from the *Brythonic*, the Welsh mother-tongue and a sister-tongue to *Latin*." IW *(trans.)*

Mellte = river name, prob. < a pers. name Mellte/Melltau, also in *Bod Mellte,* (Bedwellty) [TAG. 148]. *Bod Mellte* changed to *Bedwellty* by a series of mutations *Mellte > Fellte > Wellte.*

F > W in the Gwentian dial. eg. *waint* for *faint; wel* for *fel; weriad* for *arferiad; waldod* for *faldod* from orig. *maldod; llyswam* for *llysfam ; Llechwen (as in Llechwen Hall) for Llechfaen* etc. see BIBC. p10. Note also 1503 and 1650 forms for *Ystradfellte* where F > W. In s.Wales *bod* occasionally > *bed* as in *Bedwellty & Bedlinog (bod + llwynog).*

Sometimes the owner's name would follow *ystrad,* (IW), eg. *Ystrad Marchell, Ystrad Dyfodwg, Ystrad Nynnid.* The stem of 'Mellte/Melltau' is *mellt,* perhaps Welsh for lightning. 'Ifor Williams suggests another etymology in the Bulletin of the Board of Celtic Studies, 10.10.41 ie. *mell(t) = mwyn, hyfryd 'mild'.' BFR.*

Ystradfellte is recorded as the name of the parish, the church, village, mill and reservoir. Note the differences in the orthography of the name over the years. This emphasises the importance of having as many examples as possible of recorded place-names before attempting an etymology.

Other *ystrad* names signifying a river valley are:- *Ystradffin,* Carms; *Ystradgynlais,* Brecs; *Ystradowen,* Carms, Glam; *Ystrad Fflur,* Cards; *Ystrad Meurig,* Cards; *Ystrad Mynach,* Glam.; *Ystrad Rhondda,* Glam; *Ystrad Deur* (dwr),Valley Dore, Hereford, etc

Pron. uh-strad-vell-teh. Ystrad*fellt*e.

Sp. Ystradfellte.

Lit. meaning:- Valley of the river Mellte.

INDEX